S.H.A.D.E.S

SHADES HELP ADJUST

DANGEROUS EXPERIENCES

FOR SURVIVORS

SERIES: "AT THE HANDS OF THE SERVICE PROVIDER"

JOVAN~KA CONYERS

JOVAN~KA CONYERS....S.H.A.D.E.S.

Copyright © 2012 Jovan~ka Conyers

All rights reserved.

ISBN:0991051815
ISBN-13:978-0-9910518-1-6

JOVAN~KA CONYERS....S.H.A.D.E.S.

DEDICATION

FOR THOSE WHO WEAR S.H.A.D.E.S. IN TIMES OF DISTRESS AND FOR

THOSE WHO FAIL TO ACKNOWLEDGE THEM.

GETTING IN TOUCH WITH ME MIGHT NOT BE AS EASY AS ONE

MIGHT THINK...

GRIEF CAN GET DEEP...............

I'VE GOT STYLE........

JOVAN~KA CONYERS.....S.H.A.D.E.S.

WORKING FROM THE BOTTOM, UP......

CONTENTS

	ACKNOWLEDGMENTS	I
1	CHAPTER: LET ME INTRODUCE MYSELF	PG.12
2	CHAPTER: METAMORPHIC DESCRIPTION	PG.20
3	CHAPTER: HUMAN POTENTIAL	PG.25
4	CHAPTER: AN ANATOMY OF THE BIG THINKER	PG.30
5	CHAPTER: WHY? S.H.A.D.E.S.	PG.39
6	CHAPTER: S.H.A.D.E.S. OF DENIAL IN FASHION	PG.45
7	CHAPTER: PEEPERS	PG.50
8	CHAPTER: THE EXPERIENCE	PG.56
9	CHAPTER: FROZEN	PG.62
10	CHAPTER: SELF-REPAIR	PG.66
11	CHAPTER: BRAIN MATTERS	PG.70
12	CHAPTER: DEATH, VICTIMIZATION AND TWISTED REALITIES	PG.75
13	CHAPTER: LIGHT SHINES OUT OF DARKNESS	PG.85
14	CHAPTER: SHIFT AND FLOW	PG.90
15	CHAPTER: WE LIFT OUR HEADS IN THE SANCTUARY	PG.101
16	CHAPTER: WATCH YOUR STEP	PG.114
17	CHAPTER: WORKING WITH YOUR BODY	PG.118

18	CHAPTER: WHO DO YOU THINK YOU ARE NOT???	PG.123
19	CHAPTER: IF ONLY YOU BELIEVE	PG.129
20	CHAPTER: IMAGINE THAT HUEY	PG.136
21	CHAPTER: HEALTH AND FITNESS	PG.144
22	CHAPTER: I FEEL SOME TYPE OF WAY.....	PG.150
23	CHAPTER: BREAKING POINT	PG.158
24	CHAPTER: EXERCISE FOR WELLNESS	PG.161
25	CHAPTER: FORGIVENESS IS A PROCESS	PG.166
	ABOUT THE AUTHOR...	PG.170

JOVAN~KA CONYERS....S.H.A.D.E.S.

MEET ME WHERE I AM, NOT WHERE YOU WANT ME TO BE....IT

MAKES LIFE MUCH MORE SIMPLER

ACKNOWLEDGMENTS

S.H.A.D.E.S., an educational manual written for those who wear, S.H.A.D.E.S. and those who professionally engage those who wear S.H.A.D.E.S. The manual is written and authored from a S.H.A.D.E.S. wearer perspective. S.H.A.D.E.S. promotes safety and wellness on behalf of all Survivors and for future Generations.

Therefore, acknowledgement is also given to the Survivors who have survived Early Childhood Trauma, Domestic Violence, Death of Loved Ones, Victimization, and Vicarious Trauma. It is most unfortunate to have reality denied with all they have endured, nevertheless the struggle to be made Whole must continue. Perhaps through S.H.A.D.E.S. the general public and law makers can siege the opportunity to go back to the negotiation table.

S.H.A.D.E.S. truly supports Survivors of Childhood Trauma, Rape, Domestic Violence and other Trauma. The Writer/Author sharing her exposure to Trauma, Victimization, Grief associated with loss, Personal and Professional injustice in the aftermath of Trauma. S.H.A.D.E.S. educational model has its own dialogue for the purposes related to Survival, Trauma, and Recovery. S.H.A.D.E.S. further shadows a three-fold perspective when dealing with trauma.

Many people are aware that some experiences in life can be traumatizing, however they might not be aware of the long-term effects. Trauma can effect interpersonal and intimate relationships. It can cause family dysfunction and multiple health conditions other than Post-Traumatic Stress Disorder.

1 CHAPTER

LET ME INTRODUCE MYSELF.....

INTRODUCTION: WHERE I AM SAFE....

I stand at a distance wearing S.H.A.D.E.S that has kept me safe. There is a darkness to my path and S.H.A.D.E.S. is the safest place for me to continue my existence. I've walked amongst the shadows of gloom that has darkened life, as I know it. It's not safe to assume a person knows me without speaking with me. I have been known to speak and share my identity and self with others. Sharing bits and pieces of self is no trivial thing and its usually my Loved Ones that can identify my struggles.

I have lived a life of a solitude from a very young age and enjoy my personal space. At any given time I might walk amongst the shadows of darkness without people questioning, why. I don't like being pushed, shoved, probed, tempered with or touched without my permission. Boundaries whether Personal or Professional are very important to me. S.H.A.D.E.S. have also petitioned boundaries for my safety as I walk amongst the shadows of darkness. It is in this darkness where "The Enemies of My Household" dwell. I generally don't and won't reveal myself to "The Enemies of My Household" though I am people friendly. And for this reason there are many opinions and guesstimations about my identity and my past. Therefore, don't press what is not privy to your knowledge and don't assume my truth is your truth. S.H.A.D.E.S. protects me from compromising speakers and innuendos such as these.

Yes, profiles are sometime hard to imagine and drafts are questionable for the outsider. Many have tried to identify and many have mistaken my identity behind S.H.A.D.E.S. without asking. Quite often it starts or begins with "The Enemies of My Household. It should matter, how I feel or respond to "The Enemies of My Household." It should matter, how people, places or things became "The Enemies of My Household." It should matter, how "The Enemies of My Household" creeps or dwells amongst me. It should matter, that familial violence is "The Enemy of My Household" and that I know it by name.

S.H.A.D.E.S. is the paramount foundation to my personal SAFETY, the platform that applies to Self and Others. Through S.H.A.D.E.S. I can interact with people and the world at a distance without touching layers of pain. The mechanism has been the tool to cope, while supporting the bandages of Self Repair during a painful occurrences. My S.H.A.D.E.S. were implemented without warning and never meant for long-term protection. It is necessary for my life behind S.H.A.D.E.S. to change for a healthier me. Yes, I am the me that nobody knows and some parts of me are safest without question. I know, S.H.A.D.E.S. doesn't have to be the only mechanism of protection that promotes my longevity.

Therefore healthy tools and techniques must be implemented and my S.H.A.D.E.S. minimized. Safety is still the foundation when resetting what has been disturbed, disrupted, and distorted the view behind the S.H.A.D.E.S. The perpetrator of my S.H.A.D.E.S. has to be addressed. Self care and genuine support from others can further release the trauma that cultivated S.H.A.D.E.S. Now, with this being said, where are my options? And yet still, where am I safe?

The utmost respect and consideration must be given to a person's personal safety. There has to be a foundation built on *SAFETY*, where Hope, Love, Sensitivity, and Trust can forge a union with Self in Love. Working through distressing *EMOTIONS* acquainted with pain and trauma might be difficult however, it can be done. S.H.A.D.E.S. has closed off memories that might to come to the forefront without warning. Some memories might be so traumatic they might not be clearly understood. These memories represent threats, violence, and some things that have acquainted the Survivor with Grief. Processing and letting go must be handled with **CARE** and *CAUTION.* Closed off memories can cause Emotional upheaval, Distress, and Psychological Flashbacks. These memories could cause someone to hurt Self or Others. Therefore take heed to the cautions and remember the Survivor's Experience is painful and valid.

Picking of the pieces and assembling life as they see it, know it, believe it, and want to live it, is no easy task. Nevertheless, Cognitive-Behavioral solutions and Education has a way of giving insight behind S.H.A.D.E.S. Nothing happens overnight as we will find in the various topics that outline a "Process in Stages". The Stages help to acknowledge what we need to recognize and avoid when opening the vision. It also helps Survivor to establish goals that are applicable to revealing themselves without some, if not all of the prominent memories behind the S.H.A.D.E.S. blocking their view.

Each Survivor is different and we don't know the type of hurt thus we place a focus on education. We can trust that many Survivors have trauma child abuse histories. And there are those with traumatic childhood histories that aren't child abuse or neglect related. S.H.A.D.E.S. promotes the health and wealth of Survivors while revealing itself.

S.H.A.D.E.S. introduces various topics related to Stress, Emotions and the Experience as it offers an explanation. Not all coping mechanisms are harmful, for some it may be a matter of adjusting the lens. Body sensors support part of our abilities to function and are just as important as Emotions and other dimensions. Body Agents are physical structures, parts, and sensors that formulated the S.H.A.D.E.S. to protect the MIND of the Survivor.

S.HA.D.E.S. is working from the perspective of Denial because of the **CULTURE OF DISBELIEF.** A pattern of thinking and approaching what has continued to laden a progressively growing population with bias, rejection and intensifying a stigma. Using phases

and statements such as; "Get over it", "That's just another excuse", and "That happened so,

long ago." However, every experience of pain, trauma, and disappointment is subjective to the person behind the S.H.A.D.E.S. And their personal experience shouldn't be denied. The perspective is further more the person's right to reveal from their interpretation faulty or not.

Those that wear S.H.A.D.E.S. can expect to find their Peaks of highs, lows, and human potential. Assessing one's own skills can motivate, strengthen and encourage the Survivor living in an altered state. It is the body that has produced a protective device that has reinforced the safety of the Survivor. And because it has always been about safety we must proceed with safety.

Denial will appear in this literature to be a form of a dissociation protective mechanism. Be mindful there is a mental health diagnosis dissociative disorder and the dissociation that S.H.A.D.E.S is referencing just means to separate from in order to cope. In addition to dissociate supports a form of protection. S.H.A.D.E.S is revealing a function that is an automatic human response. However, it is possible to suffer physical, psychological and emotional long-term effects. There may be other mental health terminology nevertheless, the Author is not a mental health provider nor is she giving a mental health diagnosis. Though the explanations are helpful for those who work with people wearing S.H.A.D.E.S., to measure a situation. It is furthermore, healthier for a Survivor to promote their own personal safety and create personal space.

Boundaries create a Safe Personal Space where you can seek Refuge. It's a place that secures your Self personally and gives you Privacy. It's a place where you can learn to be Yourself and learn about Yourself. It's a Place where you prevent yourself from being in harm's way. It's a place that is absolutely yours. It's a space that gives you what you need when you need it. It's a Space and a Place that YOU have to maintain and keep secure for it is your safe space, that Separates You from Others. It is a place where you can Know Yourself and Love Yourself without interference from Anyone else. It's a place where you can assess and establish what you like and what you don't like. It's a place where you can assess and establish what you want and what you don't want. It's a place where You can be Yourself. It's the place where you take charge.

HEALTHY DEFENSES:

- ♦ Create your Safe Space
- ♦ Make healthy Choices
- ♦ Establish and Maintain a Healthier YOU

There are times in every person's life that S.H.A.D.E.S. can avail themselves. There isn't a person alive that hasn't viewed S.H.A.D.E.S., at one time or another in life. We are humans that experience pain on different levels at different times in our lives. It is most unfortunate that life has unexpected, heartbreaking experiences and events that we cannot handle. Life in itself has experiences that baffle the human mind which has its own defenses. It can leave life caught up in the process, especially when the experience leaves someone feeling broken inside and unexpectedly grieved. This is not to say that life is traumatic, but the fact is that people die, people are hurt, and some people are just mean spirited. There are also happenings that just can't be explained. There are some occurrences that catch us completely off guard. There are circumstances that we are powerless over. And there are situations that no matter how prepared, the pain is overwhelmingly unbearable. S.H.A.D.E.S. delivers us through those moments. However, we are never meant to be kept in S.H.A.D.E.S., throughout life's processes.

There are people who are not childhood trauma survivors that are identified in S.H.A.D.E.S. We have to consider people in adulthood who have overwhelming life experiences that caused them to S.H.A.D.E.S. Regardless of the facts, whether a natural disaster or man-made, the human response is not always the same as the physiological change. The body shall do a transformation that promotes Flight, Fight, or Freeze for preservation of an individual.

The S.H.A.D.E.S. population has every probability of aggressively growing at an alarming rate. We can make such a statement because of incidents such as:

- 1999 Columbine High School mass shooting, 15 killed and 24 injured
- 2007 Virginia Tech 32 people killed
- 2012 Sandy Hooks Elementary School, 20 children and 6 adult shot and killed
- 2012 Aurora Movie Theater mass shooting, 12 killed and 59 injured

There are other massacres and fatal shooting that have occurred however the point is these are not everyday occurrences. The collateral damage can leave lives unstable for many who experience the grief and the pain of such an incidents.

Man-made disaster would rank top of the list. The thought of the Hand of another human being deliberately, viciously, and maliciously participating in an atrocity. Something that is design to destroy masses of people, can be shocking. The greatest of the devastating factors may be connected to the relationship with the Hand that executes such a plan, intentionally and unintentionally. Relationships amongst Human Being are; personal, intimate, professional, neighborly all tied into family and community. There are some things that the Mind has an inability to accept from these relationships because of the nature of who these people are. S.H.A.D.E.S., scientific researcher, medical professionals and those that work within the mental health profession has attested that; Intentional Human harm and destruction from another Human Being such as those on the list below are known as some of the worst that afflict the human mind.

- Terrorism which includes Kidnapping, Hostage taking, Cult Abuse
- Torture which includes Spiritual Abuse and Cruelty
- Multiple types of Abuse including; sexual, emotional and physical
- Criminal Assaults which includes family violence, robbery, rapes
- Witnessing the harm to another which includes suicide, homicide, battering
- Military exposure to war, prisoner of war, bombing,
- Extremist behaviors such as mass murdering, ethnic cleansing

These are horrific Intentional actions to cause deliberate harm to another Human Being. These are about the worst in comparison to Accidental disaster and Acts of Nature, which some choose to call Acts of God. Scientific evidence has proven that peoples' response to acts that are accidental yet catastrophic and those attributed as acts of God, are easier to accept.

It is the hope that through S.H.A.D.E.S. many would acquire an in-depth look into the experience of survivors. It is also our hope that S.H.A.D.E.S. will provide an understanding of pain, denial, fear, stressors, and emotions from a Survivor standpoint. S.H.A.D.E.S. desires to motivate those struggling through violence to move forward and to speak the truth of pain to empower themselves.

NOTES:

2 CHAPTER

THE METAMORPHIC DESCRIPTION

If we were walking in a heat wave of 110 degrees with 98 degrees in the shade, just thinking about shade makes things cooler in the bursting heat rays of the sun is a comfort. This temperature excludes the level of environmental humidity that may add to the heat and moisture of the moment. The shade protects and creates an atmosphere that makes things much more bearable in the heat of a stressful situation. Shielded behind S.H.A.D.E.S. represents a place of comfort and a visual aide. S.H.A.D.E.S. offers so much when considering life's unexpected and unfortunate experiences.

S.H.A.D.E.S. lenses envision the experience in hostile environments and extremely stressful situations such as home or work and community. The medicated lenses are automatically adjusted to inside and outside environments. The lens tints are in reality at a peek-a-boo level. The adjustment has a critical effect just as; Home, work, and community. Therefore, we must start with these three environments first and then discuss other impacts because home, work, and community will always impact each other.

Whether life at home is stressful and spills over to work or whether work is stressful and spills over into home or whether community is having a monumental effect; Reality is the lenses must be adjusted by the survivor entering these environments. The spillage from home, work, and community have astronomical impact as the effects spill out into the social structure. S.H.A.D.E.S. frames the optical in a way that the designing views are receptively able to understand from the other side. Behind the lenses is a mechanism that withhold the forces contained in the experience that has placed one in distress.

When seeking to understand the Lenses its necessary to know that LENSES are a transparent device used to converge or diverge transmitted light to form an image. S.H.A.D.E.S. lenses function on the same axis of coming together or moving away from the snapshot of trauma. Therefore, the axis of imaginary coordinates the body rotation that aligns the image and gives focus to the visual aid. More or less it's the same process of the Occipital Body Agents of the brain. A question could be; How much physiological distress is focused?

S.H.A.D.E.S. creatively fosters a sense of strength in the struggle with experience and identity. The arms are the handles that support the psychological and emotional comfort with some form of balance. The stop post that upholds the S.H.A.D.E.S. upon the bridge of the nose support boundaries as the Euphrates Rivers of tears is restrained.

In acknowledging strength of a Survivor we equate with Euphrates River which is a stretched out place. And the Euphrates River is a good, abounding and bountiful place. Furthermore, it has a long flowing history that stretches from its location in Southwest Asia moving through Turkey into Syria and Iraq where it joins the Tigris River to form Shatt-Al-Arab near the Persian Gulf. The Euphrates has always been associated with goodness, greatness and sweetness as it has its connection with Paradise in a covenant relationship. As the Euphrates River has its shape and form, the frame shapes the world in which the survivor relates to the outside world. The outflow of the river has its comparison to the Survivor stretched out life that is maladaptive and flexible environmentally.

Home environment and familial relationships can have an impact like no other, breeding social problem. In the same respect work environments can be so impacting in relation to workplace violence. It is most unfortunate that Survivors have learned to live and function within a hostile environment.

S.H.A.D.E.S. for all appearances presents a false positive image of life being all right with me. As we explore, close doors, and open closed windows from the prescription of S.H.A.D.E.S. our outlook will be adjusted from home to the outside world. A relationship with the person behind S.H.A.D.E.S. can be fostered to impart knowledge and wisdom to know that appearance can be tricky. The person can seem to be well groomed, polite, and appear sincere or even savvy; however, it's all a front for safety. Some of the savviest of people wear S.H.A.D.E.S. and you would never guess. Talk about appearances being tricky.

The very emotional and psychological conditioning of the person can be amazing to the eyes of the outside world. After a while the person behind the S.H.A.D.E.S. is also prone to believe what is not real is real. Reminds you of; "as a man thinks so, he is." Medicated and Hostile homes, workplaces and communities can have a critical effect on all around. Therefore, we start with what hits close to home that opens doors to the effects of the environmental interacting with the physical. The _affects_ resonate with the emotional, psychological and physiological change in the person behind the S.H.A.DE.S. A Survivor might present with an indication of hard to reach persons. The presentation is struggling with what has been too traumatic to accepted.

The survivor's focus and belief are altered for comfort because they are unable to deal with reality. Some S.H.A.D.E.S. wearer can experience hardwiring through the affects of conditioning in the path of everyday life occurrences while behind the S.H.A.D.E.S. The S.H.A.D.E.S. incorporates a belief system of strength for the survivor, which will have an effect on their faith and spirit person. A stronghold can also exist which explains a grip often recognized and associate with the disease of addiction.

What is manifested in the natural can have a domino effect so safety must be paramount. There are times where the Survivor only believes that which can be seen in the lenses. This can be for a few reasons such as; the progression of denial in the perception. The inability to trust their natural instance, intuition or inner voice that warns. And wrong information that conflicts with their experiences. We see these instances in substance abuser, survivors of rape, trauma survivors, childhood sexual abuse survivors and ordinary grieving people.

Trauma breaches the building blocks of life and sometimes creates unsafe space when abandonment and broken trust unfold. These are building blocks not just supported through a bonding process, but through the Limbic System. A Body Agent that aids in the development of the brain. Abandonment is relative to levels of betrayal, emotions and unnatural violence that S.H.A.D.E.S. must adjust the eyes for survival. The depth rest within the relationship between the survivor and who or what caused the pain or distress.

Survivors hold passion and greatness within their hearts if only they could remove the S.H.A.D.E.S. and share the light with others. These hopes can change darkness to light, sadness to joy, and pain to glory. Survivors' comprehension contains an unknown desire to thrive against the greatest of enemy elements of family, community and environment. Family is the first focal point to environmentally impact because they have a way of impacting its members in the way national disasters and strangers don't. The effect a family can have on a person can vary from broken trust to death. And the environment has an ability to play a seductive part in repetition. It is very important to understand the manifestations of Body, Mind, and Spirit with life experiences of any kind.

These manifestations are also revealed through society which doesn't always have open doors. Quite frankly there are members of society that are impacting the Survivor through bias. Therefore, community attitudes and behaviors that impact; Mind, Body and Spirit can be adjusted via learning from the vision. S.H.A.D.E.S. will help with the understanding of, behaviors, attitudes and what has manifested and why. The behavior shares the actions of; the survivor, family and community that are interacting and who are in need of adjusting. Attitude shares a response that is not always understood or favorable amongst family and community who are in need of adjusting as much as the person behind the S.H.A.D.E.S.

NOTES:_____

_____

_____

_____

_____

_____

_____

_____

_____

3 CHAPTER

THE HUMAN POTENTIAL

The Eyes are the windows to the Soul and the Heart the place from where the issues of life flow. Releasing of tears affords the soul to cleanse itself of the emotional toxicities that have been pinned up. Heartache can tear into a person's soul causing heartbreak. Therefore, the tear ducts of; The Mind, Body and Spirit want to be understood for a soul cleansing experience.

The Mind, Body and Spirit are; the three concepts commonly used to break down compositions of man. There are professions that work with the Mind who understand that the three aspects must be acknowledged in resolving inner human conflict.

However, for a greater understanding of S.H.A.D.E.S. and the human potential whether man or woman there are other dimension; Spiritual, Physical, Intellectual, Emotional, Sexual, Environmental, Relational, Creative, Social, Recreational, Laborer, Cultural, Imaginative, Worshiper and Harvester. These dimensions leave a psychological and emotional impression in the individual body that has S.H.A.D.E.S. attached. S.H.A.D.E.S. has implemented an outline from which we will gain inspirational knowledge and understanding about human development and human potential. The 14 dimensions written in S.H.A.D.E.S. are given for insight and empowerment of how we are wonderfully and creatively designed.

The human mind operating in denial is impacting all levels recognized in Mind, Body and Spirit. Therefore, we have an uneven core. What S.H.A.D.E.S. is going to show is how the other areas correspond to trauma and grief with denial creating a healthy safe place for a time. In understanding how the individual dimensions function to cause a developing pathology we must look closer. We must be as Leonard De Vinci whom many know as a talented artist that became passionate and curious about the making of man, therefore, he explored through the medical world. He in fact autopsies one corpse after another by which he passed knowledge medically onto future generations through art.

The formulated information used to provide the definitions of the dimensions are the resources gathered from; Webster's Dictionary, Psychology edification, New Translation Dictionary, and Concordance Dictionary.

SPIRITUAL: of the Spirit or the Soul as distinguished from the body or material matter. That which originates from God or pertaining to God's unique image in the Universe and operates within the spiritual and physical realm.

PHYSICAL: the body, the natural, material and that which is tangible verses the intangible such as Spirit. And also refers to that which can be touched.

ENVIRONMENTAL: the area or place or surrounding of conditions, circumstances, and influences that affect the development of an organism or group of organism.

WORSHIPER: to show reverence for; to have an intense love or admiration for as a deity. Worship is interconnected within our belief system accessing a higher plain in spiritual nature whether natural or un-natural. It fosters a bowing of oneness with something.

INTELLECTUAL: pertaining to the intellect which refers to the mind, mental ability and understanding.

EMOTIONAL: responds to emotions or feelings, whether anger or pleasure.

RELATIONAL: a quality or state of being connected or related; as in thought or meaning. Connections or dealings between or amongst persons in business and private affairs. Referring of an act or proceeding to a time before its completion or enactment, as the time of its taking effect. These connections vary in relativeness, association, and related states.

SOCIAL: interactive relationships with others and relates to people living together as a group in a situation in which their dealing with one another affect their common welfare.

SEXUAL: of characteristic of or involving sex as people we are created to reproduce. And the sexuality is impacted whether male or female, or role in accordance to gender.

CREATIVE: having or showing imagination and artistic or intellectual inventiveness.

RECREATIONAL: having to do with leisure, relaxation and entertainment.

HARVESTER: that which is produced from a combination of talents, gifts, labor that is involved in his works. The works may be that in simple which is reaped from daily living or that of a profession.

IMAGINATIVE: the act or power of creating mental images of what has been actually experienced, or of creating new images, ideas, by combining pervious experiences; creative power. Anything imagined; Mental image; creation of the mind; fancy.

CULTURAL: of or pertaining to the specifics of training and refinement of the mind, interest, skills, art, etc obtaining by fostering relationships and development.

LABORER: a person who works to bring forth materials that are wage-earning. The persons' work is characterized largely by physical exertion which can be skilled or unskilled.

The above outline of the human composition provides a brief description of male or female. It is the functioning abilities of all human beings in positioned dimensions. As functioning beings in human nature the dimensions interact at all time and doesn't necessarily maintain balance without a conscious effort. Before anyone amongst us reaches for perfection its best to know it is something beyond us in the earth's realm. However, there is a nurturing of the dimensions that causes transformation within the Body, Mind and Spirit.

S.H.A.D.E.S. is preparing you for the ability to help Self and Others through the awareness of the human composition. It is essential to understand there are Natural and Spiritual law realms that affect all people. And this is not only known to; The Faith or Religious Community but, has been acknowledged through Science and Research, the medical profession and mental health profession.

As humans with emotions and intellect we have the ability to conform to S.H.A.D.E.S. upon environmentally negative impact. There is none amongst us that hasn't and doesn't use some form of denial. Denial kicks in when we are really hurting. It's the Shock Absorber for the Soul. It surrounds the heat that is generated by the Stress. We all use denial because no matter who we are; there are evils, disappointments and life experience that we are unable to readily accept. Why? Because they represent some degree of pain, fear, anger and grief. Therefore we mourn needing something to help us in living with and through the experience. And for the truly Spiritual One, note that God imparted the helping defense mechanism in the creation of man. That help comes in the S.H.A.D.E.S. of denial that follows through resiliency and coping skills.

NOTES:

4 CHAPTER

AN ANATOMY OF THE BIG THINKER

The human potential has lightly educated us on the dimensions that create the human species. We learned that we are spiritual beings that are manifested in the physical. Body, Mind and Spirit are combined concepts that are readily shared amongst people in society. The making of an anatomy requires that the Mind (Soul) to design the housing of the Spirit. Through the interactions of the soul and spirit; character, personality or persona is formed. The human spirit is one of the most powerful aspects of man as it speaks to or represents who they are.

Often a person that has experienced trauma is not in-touch with Self yet has an acquaintance in the aftermath. Therefore, it might be necessary to get involved with Self as it correlates to who you are and how the body works. The Mind inhibits the brain and during trauma the body experiences physiological changes triggered by the brain. In order to understand trauma and its physiological changes it is necessary to explore the functioning of the brain to make sense of what's going on within the Mind and Body.

The brain is supreme in structure and function and a major organ. It controls the center of the body and most superior areas of the Central Nervous System (CNS). Our brain takes control of many internal involuntary functions that we cannot control. As well as, experiences that have the ability to threaten the body and soul. When the brain responds to trauma it is responding to an extremely overwhelming stressful situation that represents danger or threats of danger.

When exploring the brain structure there are a number of parts which S.H.A.D.E.S. refers to as Body Agents. These Body Agents have a specific functions which are regulatory in purpose. They are also responsible for protecting and communicating reactions to thoughts and perils as well as human bodily functions. The three main structures of the brain are the Brain Stem, Cerebral Cortex, and the Limbic System. These are Body Agents that are responsible for directing responses to trauma and distress.

The Body Agents are responsible for preservation and survival which can have primitive reactions. The most primitive Body Agent is the **BRAIN STEM** which has the primary task of promoting survival, controlling the basic regulatory functions, organizing and assisting in regulating the rest of the brain. This Body Agent also controls, body temperature, blood pressure, heart rate, and automatically responds to threats. However, in its primitive role it's not as flexible as the other two Body Agents the Limbic or Cerebral Cortex. It's the most resistant to change and doesn't think, it only reacts.

THE LIMBIC SYSTEM: the Body Agent that is primarily linked to controlling emotion, memories and arousal. This Particular Body Agent is far more adaptable to change as it deals with the emotional state that changes more readily in comparison to the adaptability of the Brain Stem. Emotions aren't the only task of the Limbic. It's also involved with Long-Term Memory, Motivation, Self Preservation, and Relationship Building. It is further comprised of another group of Body Agents namely; the Thalamus, Hypothalamus, Amygdala, and Hippocampus which have specific tasks to perform.

THE THALAMUS: is another regulatory Body Agent where most of the Sensory input enters and distributes its data throughout the rest of the body. Just beneath is the HYPOTHALAMUS, the Body Agent, is involved with the body's homeostasis (balance), controls the autonomic nervous system (ANS), circadian rhythms, emotions, hunger and thirst. Once again there are some Body Agents that share in the function of other Body Agents. Here we have Emotions and the Autonomic System (heart rate, breathing, body temperature etc.) involved with the Hypothalamus. However, it also release hormones related to the function of the pituitary gland which is the major endocrine responsible for controlling the growth, development and functioning of other endocrines.

When it comes to trauma and threats of danger the Amygdala and the Hippocampus play a critical part in responding to the emergency. THE AMYGDALA is key, it has only one task and that's to sense danger and sound the Body Alarms. Which causes a chain of reaction and immediately all functions that aren't imperative to survival are shut off. Blood and Oxygen are sent to the muscles and adrenaline moves full force through the body. The Body is now in Self Preservation mode where there are three possible responses Fight, Flight, or Freeze. The primitive Body Agent (Brain Stem aka Reptilian Brain) has taken control of the situation. Our HIPPOCAMPUS, the base where memories are stored also kicks in and stops storing memories and start releasing cortisol. The cortisol is released to prevent one from feeling pain and allows them to focus purely on survival.

It is helpful to know that the brain has several Cortex and Lobes areas structures for separate and shared functioning.

THE CEREBRAL CORTEX is the largest part of the brain which is divided into two connected halves known as the right and left hemispheres. The right hemisphere controls the left side of the body and the left side controls the right side of the body. Generally, speaking the Cerebral Cortex in its four divisions are referred to as lobes where information is processed.

SENSORY CORTEX: responds to heat, pain, and other sensations.

MOTOR CORTEX: responsible for movement

The lobes have their responsibilities and responses to internal and external environments.

FRONTAL LOBE: (Front Portion)-- is comprised of two regions the motor and prefrontal. The motor region's responsibility communicates body movement and the prefrontal is responsible for thinking, analytic for problem solves, coordinates and directs all other areas of the brain.

PARIETAL LOBE: (Top Portion)--often we don't think of ourselves as functioning environmentally in a three dimensional space. The Parietal lobe has several responsibilities; Spatial processing happens in the parietal lobe communicating coordination and navigating in the three dimensional environmental space. It help with locating the distance of where something is located i.e. the location of a object within reach. There is also sensory functions related to Somatosensory Cortex associated with the sense of feel related to touch, pressure, temperature and pain. These feeling are not associated with emotions which are communicated through the Limbic System.

OCCIPITAL LOBE: (Back Portion)--has the responsibilities of processing functions in the visual pathway. The lobe processes and communicates vision of what is before the eyes through the Occipital.

TEMPORAL LOBE: (Bottom Side Portion) – responsible for processing auditory signals (sound).

Within the confines of two of the lobes are Language and Speech Agents. The Wernikes Area which is located in the temporal lobe and the Broca's area located in the frontal lobe. The Broca's Area named after Neurologist, Paul Broca who discovered the connection.

THE BROCA'S AREA:

USE: Speech assembly, merges sounds into words, processing language reception and comprehension.

WORK: It contains the motor neurons involved in the management of speech.

LOCATION: Left Hemisphere of the brain.

THE WERNIKES AREA:

USE: Assembles what a person wants to say

WORK: sends arrangement of speech to the Broca's Area, then speech is executed via the vocal mechanism. Thus it controls motor task involved with speech assembly enabling the created expression of speech.

LOCATION: Left Hemisphere of the brain.

The fore mentioned related to speech and the spoken words are just some of what the Broca's Area and Wernikes produces. However, people also read and listen for communication and the two areas are responsible for engaging, interacting and interpreting.

HEARING THE WORDS-begins with the auditory cortex for the processing of sound, Wernike assembles the task, relays to the Broca, which then creates the speech to be executed via the vocal mechanism.

THE WRITTEN WORDS-begins with the visual cortex for processing of text, the angular gyrus formulates a code and dispatches to Wernike for creation of what is to be spoken. Afterwards the Broca is notified to create the speech and then dispatches to the motor cortex.

However there is a condition called Aphasia that can exist when the either the Wernike or Broca's Area is damaged. The conditions vary to the point that it is easily conceived which language and speech agents are affected.

APHASIA—loss of ability to understand or express speech caused by brain damage. It's a language and speech impairment

WERNIKE APHASIA—also known as Receptive Aphasia, Fluent Aphasia, or Sensory Aphasia is a condition in which a person has an inability to understand the language in its written or spoken dialogue.

BROCA'S APHASIA—an impairment that causes difficulty when putting words together to make a sentence. The person knows what they want to say, however has troubling verbally expressing. Broca's Aphasia can occur when there is damage to the frontal area of the left hemisphere.

Though this is basic Brain Science its helpful to know trauma and other possible life experiences, can leave us with the understanding that we are shattered. Throughout S.HA.D.E.S. we will revisit the Body Agents that has supported our survival when we thought we had no help. There are also some Survivors that might be interested in knowing exactly what has physiologically happened and basic brain science can give them some answers. And the Author/Writer implements her personal experience to support the understanding of the reader and other survivors. She believes it to be helpful to identify the internal and external reactions to Traumatic life experiences and the aftermath of an horrendous occurrence. The body and the mind are readily focused on the Survivors primary preservation during these times.

S.H.A.D.E.S. shields the position just right to adjust the light impacting the human emotions and physiological changes. On a sunny day a person can be at home or work and adjust the window covering to let in just the right amount of light needed. S.H.A.D.E.S. conversion simplifies to demonstrate the versatility of denial and soul which correlates to the human mind. The designed covering denotes the mystery and intrigue of a veil of what has occurred in the life experience of a Survivor.

A person must be careful with the positioning of the shields and how the light enters. Because of what's at stake here "the Mind / Soul." And with the Mind who can truly understand it? Therefore, steps of safety, acknowledgment of the pain, compassion with dignity creates trust. We are going to look into some housing developments under construction behind S.H.A.D.E.S. While, we are going through the progress and potential remember the meaning of the acronym S.H.A.D.E.S. "Shades Helps Adjust Dangerous Experiences for Survivors." Regardless, of what has occurred strength must be given to the Survivor who has possibly had multiple experiences. The Survivors needs to know the reality of surviving what some others didn't make it through.

It's time to explore some other factors and aspects of the anatomy that places emphasis on the reactions of the person behind the S.H.A.D.E.S. Because the body has been partitioned unto a tremendous strain to survive. People are physical beings that can be environmentally impacted. The body has a way of responding to antagonist and knows what actions it should take. Our anatomy has physical properties that are tangible and has body agents that are chemical. Whether inside or outside the anatomy, the effects are environmental, meaning internal and external. Though the environmental is internal and external whereas the physical is only external despite the tangible properties of the internal.

PHYSICAL: the body, the natural, material and that which is tangible verses the intangible such as Spirit. And also refers to that which can be touched.

ENVIRONMENTAL: the area or place or surrounding of conditions, circumstances, and influences that affect the development of an organism or group of organism.

S.H.A.D.E.S. has spoken of the emotional response to extremely stressful violence however, there is a need to focus on the Body Agents of the anatomy. Many are knowledgeable about the effects of; neurotransmitters, hormones, and other chemical messengers that are effective in influencing Memory, Mood, and Emotional Balance. These Body Agents work from the internal to the external and respond to external environmental affects.

When the Body Agents malfunction there can be extenuating responses to the proper manner in which they are to function. The person behind the S.H.A.D.E.S. should become aware of the body and how it works from the internal. It can help them recognize consciously and identify with their feelings which are a sub division of the Emotions. Working with their body can best benefit them when becoming aware of triggers that could cause them to neglect themselves or relapse into old behaviors. Working with the body has its pros and cons for the person behind the S.H.A.D.E.S. And therefore when deemed necessary they should always work through the new task with a counselor, mental health professional, and primary care physician.

NOTES:_____

_____
_____
_____
_____
_____
_____
_____
_____
_____
_____
_____
_____
_____
_____
_____
_____
_____
_____
_____

5 CHAPTER

WHY? S.H.A.D.E.S.

Previously it was said, *"There isn't a person alive that hasn't viewed S.H.A.D.ES."* for the most part we are all vulnerable to Vicarious or Secondary Trauma. We also experience emotional pain, threats of violence, and loss associated with grief perspectively different. The term Vicarious Trauma is also known as Secondary Trauma. Therefore, when we are refocused behind S.H.A.D.E.S. through Vicarious Trauma (VT), its traumatizing empathic engagement. This is where a person is exposed to devastation, horrendous catastrophe, terrorism, assault victims, trauma survivors experience, etc. as First Responders, Worker, or Helper (Peepers). What happens is the person imagines, witnesses, or hears the occurrence and transforms Self into the traumatic experience of another.

The Hallmark to VT is disruption of spirituality and disruption of a Workers perception of Hope. It's as though the world represents a dark and gloomy place with the worst being the end results. It can cause social withdrawal, intrusive thoughts, emotional distress and maladaptive behaviors (Self Repair).

Trauma associated with grief is very important to note because a person can have Grief without trauma. However, a person cannot have trauma without grief, as trauma also has an element of loss connected. Though grief associated with the Death of a Loved One can be traumatizing, as is the witnessing of death related to empathic engagement mentioned above. Therefore, we know grief can also be traumatizing in someone's personal and professional life, depending on the nature of the relationship, the cause of death, and whether its unexpected. As with other forms of trauma it's still subjective in depth and effects.

Constant **NEGLECT** and **ABUSE** as in the Author/ Writer's experience can eventually share the attributes of Trauma and be the primary contributing fact. A failure to respond to her impacted the needs of her children and unstabilized of her household.

S.H.A.D.E.S. defines some prominent meanings related to Trauma;

1. **TRAUMA**---is a emotional response to a terrible event like an accident, rape or natural disaster. Immediately after the event, shock and denial are typical. Longer term reactions include unpredictable emotions, flashbacks, strained relationships and even physical symptoms such as headaches and nausea. in accordance to the American Psychological Association

2. **PSYCHOLOGICAL TRAUMA**—is a type of damage to the psyche that occurs as the result of a severely distressing event. Trauma, which means injury in Greek, is often the result of an overwhelming amount of stress that exceeds one own ability to cope or integrate the emotions involved with the experience.

3. **PHYSICAL TRAUMA**--according to Science Daily refers to a physical injury. In medicine, however the word Trauma Patient usually refers to someone who has suffered serious and life-threatening physical injury potentially resulting in secondary complications such as; shock, respiratory failure and death.

4. **POST-TRAUMATIC STRESS DISORDER (PTSD)**—The National Institution of Mental Health (NIMH) states. "Anyone can get PTSD at any age. This includes war veteran

and survivors of physical and sexual assault, abuse, accidents, disasters, and many other serious events. Not everyone with PTSD has been through a dangerous event. Some people get PTSD after a friend or family member experiences danger or is harmed."

5. **SITUATIONAL TRAUMA**— Extremely stressful events, causes are man-made in the form of abuse and violence. Though the trauma can also be related to natural disasters, war and accidents.

S.H.A.D.E.S.'s educational objective is to develop an understanding of Trauma, Impact and Recovery throughout the manual. S.HA.D.E.S. finds a median for the Survivor to function in their everyday life in the aftermath. It's not only comfortable, it's a safe place, it provides privacy and gives the ability to cover the wound that has penetrated on a level that overwhelms sensibility. S.H.A.D.E.S. shelter of protection has the similarity to a myopic view. Which is an abnormal eye condition where the light fails to focus on the retina causing a narrow view of things. Therefore, objects are not seen distinctly or what can be best referred to as a lack of sight collaborating the confirming truth in the words of Kathleen J. Moroz;

"If Clinicians fail to look through a trauma lens and to conceptualize client problems as related possibly to current or past trauma, they may fail to see that trauma victims, young and old, organize much of their lives around repetitive patterns of reliving and warding off traumatic memories, reminders, and effects." (2005 "The Effects of Psychological Trauma on Children and Adolescents").

The person can also overcome extremely stressful circumstances and gives the ability to hide for a time. It's a mask for the pain and distress that attempts to keep all the alarms from sounding. In a later chapter on Peepers the myopic view shall be deemed supportive to those who are shortsighted. S.H.A.D.E.S. is what covers the eyes after exposure to extreme violence that stirs emotional and physiological arousal. S.H.A.D.E.S. concept of Denial is synonymous with a person wearing sunglasses. And we know that people buy them in different tints, the different frames, and the lenses may have different shapes. Sunglasses are visual aids that are used as blockers to protect the eyes from the violence of the sun *(ULTRAVIOLET RADIATION)*. Over the decades scientist and those of the medical profession have found that radiation from the sun is damaging. The ultraviolet radiation has been found harmful to the eyes and lens have a blocker (sunscreen) used to coat the lens in order to protect the eyes.

Sunglasses have also been known to hide the stars, keeping the identity from coming to light. S.H.A.D.E.S. is appealing to high profile people living their life's dreams though, they still have to protect themselves against that which could possibility hurt them. It has been their hope of not being exposed to elements that impact their lives amongst community. The Shades protect their peace to participate in Routine Activities and walk amongst the general public. Nevertheless, some Celebrities are disturbed by the public and exposed to extreme stress, violence, and other overwhelming situations that stirs the Emotions. And these are everyday possible situations that are only related to an individual's lifestyle and success that accompanies stardom.

Denial is beneficial to understand with its differences in sight and style of a person. And reality is that shades don't allow a person to be exposed to the light of day as it is. Therefore the exposure is within the range or scope of the person's ability to accept reality. They are shielded to the fact that their view of the situation doesn't conform to reality. The denial system distorts their perception and impairs their judgment so they become self-deluded and incapable of accurate self-awareness. It is to get caught up in this masquerade or fantasy or spellbound nature which can also have a trans like state. There is a saying; "To be aware is to be alive" however when dealing with denial, people aren't aware.

A person may be faced with a traumatic experience, death of a loved one, a medical issue, the disease of addiction etc. It could be anything that a person perceives to be a life and death threat. When it comes to the aspect of life it's a matter of how someone may believe their life is affected by another, situations or circumstances. For instance, Domestic Violence Survivors may have a thought within this respect that isn't related to co-dependency but starting over with perceived threats of violence, scars, and emotional pain. Whatever the issues flight, fight, and freeze has its protective S.HA.D.E.S. within the mind-blowing experience.

Denial kicks in automatically it is not a matter of deliberate lying to avoid or willful deception. Some have referred to denial as the shock absorber, however its meant to ensure the person's survival with overwhelming stress. It's not to say that there aren't instances where there is backlash of emotional responses. A perfect example would be someone that test positive for H.I.V and perceives or internalizes as death. The problem here is the person has internalized death instead of life in a survival mode.

Denial can progress unto death because the person isn't giving Self a chance to live. Some respond in self destructive ways and continued to deplete or destroy their Immune System. Some go as far as hurting other people out of fear and anger. Yet, some become uncomfortable with Self and the stigmatization related to the diagnosis and the ignorance of those around them. Modern research and technology has made life changing discoveries for the person living with H.I.V. or A.I.D.S.

Many readily accept that denial protects the person from information, situations, and circumstances that are distressingly extremely painful for them to accept. Keeping the two explanations in mind, denial is protective, progressive and a barrier to healing and recovery. It keeps the person from learning to cope with the reality they are unable to meet eye to eye.

NOTES:_____

_____

_____

_____

_____

_____

_____

_____

_____

_____

_____

_____

6 CHAPTER

S.H.A.D.E.S. OF DENIAL IN FASHION:

S.H.A.D.E.S of denial in fashion opens our eyes and mind to the different types of designer wear being worn to S.H.A.D.E. the experience. Denial has many forms as does S.H.A.D.E.S. with their creative designer wear which can be supportive or non supportive. **DENIAL OF FACT:** This form of denial is where someone avoids a fact by lying. This lying can take the form of an outright falsehood (commission), leaving out certain details in order to tailor a story (omission), or by falsely agreeing to something. Someone who is in denial of fact is typically using lies in order to avoid facts <u>that they think</u> may be potentially painful to themselves or others.

Keep in mind that person may also S.H.A.D.E because of shame based issues which is another perception on how to approach with understanding of the emotional impact. Because the person in which you are envisioning has their own perception of the truth prevailing against them. You must take into consideration how they perceive those who are involved and the exposure to the light. The matter of a shamed based issue can take someone into isolation through S.H.A.D.E.S. It can involve the person, family members or a loved one. The cover up can be catastrophic and it is imperative that one is mindful when unraveling the pain of shame based related issue. It is like this;

Think or reflect on an individual who is blind and there is a discovery after closer examination that corrective laser surgery on the eyes can bring forth the sight. Now the surgery is performed as with a person with glaucoma to restore the sight that is under a sugar coated glaze. The eyes are wrapped for the protection and the doctor must remove the bandages gently and slowly. The doctor knows the pain and danger of the light hitting the patient's eyes too quickly, without proper time to adjust. The room is also dark and the doctor's assistant opens the blinds slowly under the direction of the doctor. The Patient is also under the doctor's direction in the opening of the eyes as they are instructed to reveal the experience they are having in the recovery.

Therefore, we move through with mindfulness, knowledge, and attentive listening skills to hear what is not easily distinguished through sight and style. Familiarizing oneself with types of denial will become a valuable tool. Because there may be times when the types are over lapping. However never underestimate the pain, fear, anger and the grief of sorrow behind the S.H.A.D.E.S.

S.H.A.D.E.S. OF DENIAL

DENIAL OF FACT: This form of denial is where someone avoids a fact by lying. This lying can take the form of an outright falsehood (commission), leaving out certain details in order to tailor a story (omission), or by falsely agreeing to something. Someone who is in denial of fact is typically using lies in order to avoid facts that they think may be potentially painful to themselves or others.

DENIAL OF RESPONSIBILITY: This form of denial involves avoiding personal responsibility by blaming, minimizing or justifying. Blaming is a direct statement shifting culpability and may overlap with denial of fact. Minimizing is an attempt to make the effects or results of an action appears to be less harmful than they may actually be. Justifying is when someone takes a choice and attempts to make that choice look okay due to their perception of what is "right" in a situation. NOTE: this also has to do with the perception of the person and denial in large part is about perceptions about what the truth is and the inability to cope with and accept. Someone using denial of responsibility is usually attempting to avoid potential harm or pain by shifting attention away from them self. Many people that are addicts are unusually known for this type of denial.

DENIAL OF IMPACT: Denial of impact involves a person avoiding thinking about or understanding the harms their behavior have caused to themselves or others. By doing this, that person is able to avoid feeling a sense of guilt and it can prevent that person from developing remorse or empathy for others. Denial of impact reduces or eliminates a sense of pain or harm from poor decisions.

DENIAL OF AWARENESS: This type of denial is best discussed by looking at the concept of state dependent learning. People using this type of denial will avoid pain and harm by stating they were in a different state of awareness (such as alcohol or drug intoxication or on occasion mental health related). This type of denial often overlaps with denial of responsibility.

DENIAL OF CYCLE: Many who use this type of denial will say things such as, "it just happened." Denial of cycle is where a person avoids looking at their decisions leading up to an event or does not consider their pattern of decision making and how harmful behavior is repeated. The pain and harm being avoided by this type of denial is more of the effort needed to change the focus from a singular event to looking at preceding events. It can also serve as a way to blame or justify behavior. Always remember denial can overlap and is progressive, it can be as a winding road.

DENIAL OF DENIAL: This can be a difficult concept for many people to identify in themselves, but is a major barrier to changing hurtful behaviors. Denial of denial involves thoughts, actions and behaviors which bolster confidence that nothing needs to be changed in one's personal behavior. This form of denial typically overlaps with all of the other forms of denial, but involves more self-delusion.

Observation from the many shades of denial indicates a person can present in a tricky situation with over lapping consequences. Has anyone been able to share in the reality of S.H.A.D.E.S. and develop an understanding of the person? Yes, the Peepers. Although all Peepers are not able to deal with S.H.A.D.E.S. Denial can be prevalent in a dual relationship. The person in hiding seeking assistance and the Peeper that refuses them can both be in denial.

One thing for sure is there is a lot to behold within a person and the person behind the S.H.A.D.E.S. The only thing holding them back is a lack of understanding about Self, and the pain that is contained in a delayed reaction to the distressing circumstances or situations. There is a substantial amount of stress related to the grief that may very well be accompanied with anger. Stress and Anger may rise up together in an instance. On the other hand there may also be a golden moment of release from the pain that has keep them bound which is at best relief. The golden moment has the environmental elements of being released from a time capsule. Nevertheless, life for all human being has potential that could open the doors to greatness.

NOTES:

7 CHAPTER

{PEEPERS}

S.H.A.D.E.S. opens the eyes of the Peepers through the most difficult, painful and wounded parts of the past and present. The Peepers are those from the most important, influential, or caring persons in relationships of S.H.A.D.E.S. Many Peepers are in the lives of S.H.A.D.E.S. only because of the pain or consequences that are too great to endure. Some Peepers exist for the same reason, meaning they wear S.H.A.D.E.S.

Knowledge of Peepers wearing S.H.A.D.E.S. is extremely important because of the possible impact they can have on those they are positioned to help. There may be some adverse emotions that create a bias or an awkward response to persons behind the S.H.A.D.E.S. It's their personal pain that creates the response and causes them to make a wrong decision or transfer their pain of perception. Persons living behind S.H.A.D.E.S., can also transfer their pain to the Peeper creating an affliction. It could cause the "that's just an excuse" syndrome of disbelief to present itself.

Peepers can have a myopic view resulting in their shortsightedness. They either lack vision and are in need of corrective lenses or need a change in attitude concerning the Trauma Survivor. It's very unfortunate there are some Peepers who are in denial when it comes to evaluating the needs of a person wearing S.H.A.D.E.S. And because the Peeper's scope is so narrow they commit themselves into a myopic belief that they are the only ones with the ability to service Trauma Survivors. Denial of denial such as this has been demonstrated under the Department of Mental Health and Hygiene. As a result their behavior and attitude has impacted the S.H.A.D.E.S. Community directly. And this is what happened in the case of the Author/ Writer at the hands of multiple Peepers.

Trauma can be caused by an overwhelmingly negative event that causes a lasting impact on the victim's mental and emotional stability. While many sources of trauma are physically violent in nature, other are psychological. Some common sources of trauma include; Rape, Domestic Violence, Natural Disaster, Severe illness/ Injury, Death of loved one, and Witnessing an act of violence. -----PsychGuides.Com 2016.

The Author/ Writer was impacted multiple times and her trouble rest with the above statement. It lead to her experiencing one miscarriage of justice after another with victimization overlapping one traumatic experience after the other. Her children were impacted and her household disrupted by the negative behaviors and attitudes of the Peepers.

If we were to widen the scope of the myopic view it might reveal a conflict of interest that impacts the relationship between the Peeper and Survivor. Since it's a matter of a conflict of interest the problem goes deeper than a lack of knowledge or an inability to assert understanding. Though under these circumstances a Peeper might have a Survivor in years of unnecessary therapy, making wrong assumptions, and trapped in their situation.

Peepers wearing S.H.A.D.E.S. can stands to reason why they aren't able to work objectively or subjectively with the Survivor. This can lead to a disservice or undeserving in a capacity that the Peeper can cause harm. When Peepers have Trauma issues that haven't been addressed there's going to be a strong chance of situations where they; neglect, over compensate, discriminate and act with bias related to their trauma history. The trauma history can also be vicarious or secondary trauma reactions to the Survivor. And what is overwhelmingly obvious is a conflict of interest that begins to renegotiate the Peeper /Survivor relationship.

Nevertheless, times have changed and with the times, choices are abundantly great for Survivors when it comes how to deal with their trauma issue. The Writer/ Author of S.H.A.D.E.S. has used various models and technique though she has her preferences such as Instinctual Trauma Response Model, Educational Trauma Model and The Expressive Emotions Therapy Model. She has also used techniques such as relaxation, mediation, spiritual guidance, and the art of writing. And in the agreeable words of Dr. Linda Gnatt "Those with trauma related issues are those that are the most treatable and it doesn't take years to do it." Dr. Linda Gnatt an Art Therapist and her husband Dr. Louis Tinnin a Psychiatrist developed the Instinctual Trauma Response Model.

Traumatologist Margaret Vasquez also shares her educational, professional and personal experience with the Instinctual Trauma Response Model. S.H.A.D.E.S. in a later chapter shall revisit the educational application of Traumatologist, Margaret Vasquez, in correlation to the recovery experience of this manual's Author/ Writer.

Trauma is also associated with chronic health condition such as pain, anxiety, depression etc for which there is "Self Applied" treatment. The Association Awareness Technique (AAT) created by Scott Musgrave, MSPT, a Chronic Pain and Human Performance Specialist provides insight into the constant or repeated engagement of the Physiological effects of trauma and how to change the challenging cycle.

However, the message that S.H.A.D.E.S. wants to convey is hope, acceptance of the truth, feelings, and the Survivor's perception. Therefore Peepers must learn to take care of themselves in the midst. It isn't necessary to disclose as the Author/Writer of S.H.A.D.E.S. A Peeper with or without wearing S.H.A.D.E.S. must establish a relationship of care. TRUST is essential to the removal the S.H.A.D.E.S. and opening the eyes. The eyes of the Survivor speak the truth that trusting after traumatic pain inflicted by people, love isn't easy. So, TRUST that replaces feeling of betrayal supports a healthy Mind, Body, and Spirit exacerbates hope. The feelings will also be substantiated through processing of what reality lies behind the S.H.A.D.E.S.

When a person engages the reality that they have a situation that they cannot handle alone, from a social aspect, Peepers may be who they choose. Though some will choose a close friend, family member, or anyone they believe could be trusted. It has further been the Author/Writers experience that a person wearing S.H.A.D.E.S. will also trust the reality of the pain they hold with a stranger. The uniqueness in speaking with a stranger is comfort in knowing somebody knows and the pain is released. It allows the Survivor to move on with their day without a burden of heart on their mind. The concept of sharing with a stranger has a similarity to journaling. A stranger represents the shortest of possibilities that you may never meet again and when journaling you don't have to share the contents until you are ready. Nevertheless, the pain, traumatic feelings, and experience are released for processing the emotions and stress. It is never a healthy situation where one is burdened with heavy laden stress that can create medical conditions.

Therefore, the adjusting device will differ from Survivor to Survivor. The adjustment device will be the choice of the survivor in helping to blend effects of uncomfortable people, places, and things. Which means the Peepers must be open-minded with the understanding that the experience is subjective and what is good for one S.H.A.D.E.S. may not be good for another. That means, you meet S.H.A.D.E.S. where they are, not where you want them to be, or where you are. It means compassion, knowledge, active listening, attentive listening with teaching tools of change that supports survivor and allows them choices.

Peeps are what S.H.A.D.E.S. allows to the outside world that forms social or service structures. The Peeps are shown to everyone from the intimate to the casual relationship. These relationships include everyone from immediate family members to the pastor. The person behind the frames grieves help in some of the most unusual ways. Peeps support a present mental and emotional state that are of reality, but are providing access to S.H.A.D.E.S. Therefore, if not for S.H.A.D.E.S. the person may live a life cut off from society's interaction on a whole. So, let us understand the S.H.A.D.E.S. are providing some hope for the survivor.

Peepers' experiences are dimmed to the future unless the knowledge concerning eyes of denial are opened. Many survivors will not make it out of an unrealistic place without intervention of some sought. Reality can be awesomely tricky since some aspects are unrealistic for the person behind the S.H.A.D.E.S. When we speak of unrealistic expectation or the unrealistic, it could work both ways in respect to the Peeper and the Survivor. Denial has many eyes of colors and forms for defenses at various times in the Survivor's life that represents safety. We are aware that there are supportive Peepers, evidence within the Mental Health and Medical Professions that validates S.H.A.D.E.S. The reality, and the public's response to effects of traumatic experiences and abusive behavior is also noted. Therefore, we have supportive visions and visual aides to assist with the removal of those somewhat dark glasses.

What S.H.A.D.E.S. wants to unveil is the long-term effect through a presumed stability of denial. And this also opens the windows and doors of the Mind and Emotion as the empowering information is filtered in through others that know it's okay to share the pain.

S.H.A.D.E.S. basis is; Experience, Survival, and Intervention for healing and recovery. And this takes COURAGE especially when the person behind the S.H.A.D.E.S. knows or suspects that BETRAYAL or GRIEF staged their course. Betrayal is best identified as a breach of TRUST in a RELATIONSHIP.

NOTES:_____

_____
_____
_____
_____
_____
_____
_____
_____
_____
_____
_____

8 CHAPTER

THE EXPERIENCE

S.H.A.D.E.S. is a matter of happenings, experiences, and events that can tremendously strain reality. There are many instances and multiple reasons why a person is wearing the S.H.A.D.E.S. Our perception of people, places, and things can be challengingly changed after trauma. And emotionally, psychologically, and a physiologically we are changed behind the S.H.A.D.E.S. Therefore, let's prepare to take a trip through an experience behind the S.H.A.D.E.S. The Author/Writer separates two groups of people in her experiences which she refers to as Co-Workers and Employees, while Staff refers to everybody. It's necessary for identification with what happened before and after the experience.

THE EXPERIENCE IN MOTION:

So, on 9/11 this Author was engaged in Routine Activities without a care in the world. She got up, prayed, showered, got dress and went to work with another agenda other than Terrorism on her Mind. Once she arrived early for work, she dropped her lunch on her desk and went to Radio Shack to price a few things for her ministry in its early stages of development. But as she turned onto Pearl Street she noticed some emergency vehicles with sirens blazing. She acknowledged them and chalked it up to someone being taken to nearby Beekman hospital.

However, after her price shopping, as she walked back onto Pearl Street she noticed things seemed a little deserted. The atmosphere gave the subtle appearance of a gloomy abandoned district with the exception of: Herself, 2 Department of Sanitation Street Cleaners and darkness that indicated a fire somewhere. The three of them questioned on to another, what was going on. The Author/Writer stated, it's a fire across town and she pointed to the debris. Paper and black smoke was surrounding the skies and was submerging on the area. It seemed as though her answer sufficed their curiosity. Therefore, she said, Have a Nice Day and she went on her way.

Lo and behold she met with one of the Employees as she re-entered the office building who stated that a helicopter crashed into The World Trade Building. Her Co-Worker and an Employee were in the office space where she worked. So, she told them; a helicopter crashed into The World Trade Building. They didn't take her serious at all and told her stop that. Then the Office Manager would go whizzing by, rushing, to his office where he had a full window view. She said, see look at him rushing to his office and they followed him to see The World Trade Building on Fire. She didn't follow them instead closed herself off and went into a single employee bathroom and prayed for the personal safety of the People and the City. Then she went and got her music and pocketbook and went to the Receptionist Desk. She was still as clueless as many around her about a Terrorist Attack.

Therefore, she went on with her day as her Co-worker and Employees continued looking through the windows. More and more windows became available for the viewing the many thought was just an accident. Employees entered their offices with their picture fame windows to such a tragic view. Still clueless she put her gospel music in the disk player and as she squatted to sit she heard her them scream. And she said, "God, now what's wrong with them?" She came from behind the Receptionist Desk and calmly walked down to the Offices. There was no room in the Office Manager's Office. So she went over to the Personnel Director's partially dark Office, where it wasn't too crowded.

However, when she went to enter she suddenly stopped at the door unable to enter for a moment. She saw from a distance where a Second plane had flown into The World Trade Office Building. She struggled to get closer to the window where she observed a male Employee standing. It was difficult because she found herself in a familiar place, standing at the door frame unable to move.

1ST RECALL: As a 4 or 5 year old child she witnessed an innocent accident which she remembered like it happened yesterday. She began recalling the experiences finer details of that evening. In the minutes prior to a fatal accident she stood at a distance at the door frame of the room. Children were piling one on top of the other in excitement while attempting to look out a window. The space had become too crowded. There was too much with pushing, shoving and excitement. She said to herself, "I'm not getting in that." She knew she too short to fit and had thought it to be dangerous. So, she glanced over and seen a window in the next room where she did fit. However, before she could move the accident she feared occurred and left her still and speechless.

Therefore, during this 9/11 experience she focused on the Employee standing at the window shadowed in semi-darkness. Focusing on him enable her to enter the office and move closer to the window. She stood somewhat behind him and glanced at The World Trade Building which was too much for her to handle. She turned around immediately leaving the Office and went to the Temp's Office Space. Inside her Coworker and an Employee were sitting at their desks. They looked at her not noticing she had been emotionally tossed and said; Are you leaving? She responded with her left index finger pointed upward at the ceiling; As soon as I find my pocketbook. They repeated are you leaving and she responded in the same poised position, as soon as I find my pocketbook.

She had two desks that she worked from and had to locate her pocketbook. First she looked over the small partition in the office where the two were sitting that questioned what she was about to do. The only thing visible was the black shopping bag that contained her lunch. She thought about picking it up but decided it wasn't that important and advised her Coworker not to just sit there on the phone, leave.

Once she located her pocketbook which she had left under the Receptionist Desk she headed toward to the stairway. She noticed one of the Employees walking back towards his desk and she called out to him by his name and when he turned to her she said, are you coming. He said, I believe I will. Some of the Employees and her Coworkers were already preparing to leave to floor. In another direction she noticed several Employees at the door trying to comfort another Employee who had become overwhelmingly upset. The Employee insisted on waiting for the instruction to come across the P.A. System. S.H.A.D.E.S. Author/Writer, her Coworker, and some Employees ran down the stair with her in the front until she froze at the door. An Employee coming up beside her push the panic bar where she could see, it was clear to exit the building.

They exited the side door and when she walked around the corner headed for the bus it was strange to see a crowd of people gawking at the sight beyond what they could see. She kept on moving until she saw an Employee entering the building and tried to stop him from entering. Nevertheless, he was forceful about the grace period as he was late for work and his greatest concern was swapping in to get paid for the time. There was no convincing him so she continued on her way and she turned the next corner onto Water Street. There were crowded Streets and a multitude standing still and some moving in one direction or another. But there was a bus at a distance so she walked down where the crowds weren't as heavy in order to assure getting out the area on the approaching bus.

It would happen to be the last number M9 bus leaving that area with no thought of the subway. There on the bus she was greeted by another Employee that she sternly reminded "If it hadn't been for God where would we be?" He without a doubt had to agree though she was never concerned with where he had placed his faith. The bus moved along its route with "The World Trading Building" visibly seen as burning beyond its original state as the bus passed under the Brooklyn Bridge. After the bus passed under the bridge her telephone service was restored and she called to check on her Daughter and Grandson. The Author/Writer got off the bus at 14 Street at 2nd Avenue with her Pocketbook.

One would wonder what was in the pocketbook. Well let's see. The Author/Writer walked into the nearest Post Office and cashed a $100.00 money order that she kept in her wallet for emergency purposes only. From her childhood she had learned that people could be unreliable. Therefore she always tried her best to keep emergency funds available for cases of emergency. And this was an emergency as it was before pay day which was obviously going to be delayed and she had no food in the apartment. The phone service plan was also running low however, she had a functioning credit card. As blessings would come the Phone Carrier provided all its customers with addition minutes to their plan to cover the emergency.

And when the storm lifted she returned to work appearing her normal Self. Right down to when she went to turn in her Time Sheet. She asked the Liaison what was going to be done about the days they weren't able to work. Ever reminding the Liaison and adamantly stating; "I am not responsible for Terrorist Attacks." The Liaison told her to take the Time Sheets to the Office Manager and have him sign them. That's exactly what she did and told him as well "I am not responsible for Terrorist Attacks." Once he signed it, she went to the Office Space and told her Coworker to give her Time Sheets to the Office Manager to sign complete with all the Time she had missed. After that was done, she took both hers and her Coworker's Time Sheets downstairs to the Liaison to be submitted to the payroll department. Bottom line they got their money as they should have. Life after a time had begun appearing to return to normal and she moved on in her everyday life.

NOTES:

9 CHAPTER

{FROZEN}

WHAT'S BEYOND THE DOOR???

Everything within her was able to speak, move and unction, to tell Staff to leave the building. Then something happened (1) A STIMULUS motivated change that stirs in the environment that impacts the nervous system. (2) A RESPONSE connected to the STIMULUS creating the REACTION. (3) An IMPULSE dispatched a message carried CHEMICALLY by nerve cells to the Central Nervous System.

Talk, about the "body speaks" and "body languages" that suggest there is some truth to the statement "I am a bundle of nerves." The statement has been used in situations where a person didn't know how to get through a STRESSFUL situation, especially one that caught them by surprise. And the Author/Write froze. She went from flight to frozen through an associated traumatic experience.

" What's beyond the Door," became the most urgent pivotal question in her mind. The question that caused her to freeze at the panic bar. At the Door, she envisioned in her Mind the danger of glass and fire falling. And she froze, in a split second she went from flight to frozen without notice. Or was she frozen all along, is really the question! Her Limbic System was releasing shut off details of childhood experiences in the 9/11 adulthood experience.

2ᴺᴰ RECALL: Her mind unveiled a very vivid picture of what was thought to be beyond the door. The thought of people running, screaming and moving to safety, dodging pass falling debris of glass and fire caused her to Freeze from what she imagined. She perceived it to be a literal war-zone beyond the doors. She was having flashbacks these were images of escaping a burning building when she was in the 3rd grade. She remembered neighbors knocking on doors making sure everyone got out. There were people watching and adults calling out in the street. A Fireman existed the building carrying her as a small piece of falling hot glass hit her foot.

Nevertheless, she returned to work in a frozen state and continue to pursue career goals. Her trauma memories were in the shadows and she wasn't maintaining her stability through Self Repair Methods. Shortly after she made a career change that would be to her benefit without thinking back on 9/11. She began taking classes with Arrive/Exponents in 2002 in learn how to support H.I.V positive people. However, one evening on the way to class she had an experience that she didn't understand. She didn't understand or could she comprehend why it happened.

3ᴿᴰ RECALL: The Author/Writer began hearing the voice of a man crying and pleading with her Mother. He sounded like he was in despair as he banged repeatedly on the door and calling out her name. He cried out in grief with the same request repeatedly in a heartbreaking way. Once again the Author/Writer found herself at the door and this time she was in tears about what had happened.

Upon arriving to class that evening the training was conducted by the Executive Director of Arrive. He taught on the disease of addiction and the Beast Within, a book he had written. It was during this particular session that the Author/Writer shared the experience and the notion that it was like a recalled memory. The Executive Director responded and told her that something happened to her and the memory had been blocked. He also said that he believed that God allowed it to reveal itself because you are now able to handle the information.

When she changed work environments and occupational status the effects of 9/11 were with her. While credentialed as an Alcohol and Substance Abuse Trainee (CASAC-T) under New York State, she continued her education. In January 2006 she engaged in a training at the New York Alcoholism Council on "Women, Substance Abuse and Post Traumatic Stress Disorder." For a small group exercise, the Facilitator, instructed the class to come up with a scenario related to Trauma and Substance Abuse.

However, the Author/Writer's small group couldn't get their short scenario together so, she told the group of her "What's Beyond the Door?" experience. Each small group had to share their story with the class. And when the experience of her Recovery during the training was revealed, the Facilitator was amazed. The reason it's considered Recovery is because she knew of her overwhelming stress, nevertheless she couldn't identify where it was coming from. Nevertheless, there was a release of the trauma related stress. The Facilitators response was "Great Scenario" until it was revealed that it was a true story related to effects of 9/11. It was the first time she had ever shared the 9/11 experience with flashbacks and was able to understand the freeze response. The feeling of overwhelming stress ceased to exist 5 years later.

And this is only the tip of an iceberg, because the Author/ Writer flashbacks are not related to 9/11. Which means that she had already been laced with trauma and began exhibiting the effects. Though many Childhood Trauma Survivors have histories of physical, sexual, and verbal abuse the experiences are subjective. Every Survivor's experience is subjective as with the Author/ Writer's whose experience speaks of other types of violence. It is also noteworthy to understand, what is classified as violence and traumatizing for the Survivor.

NOTES:_____

_____

_____

_____

_____

_____

_____

_____

_____

_____

_____

_____

_____

10 CHAPTER

SELF REPAIR

Quite often a Trauma Survivor will show up with badly bandaged wounds where they have attempted to heal through one Self-Repair after another. They show up as Substance Abusers, Suicidal, with Disabilities, as Cutters, and with Internalized Anger, etc. And for one reason or another they fall apart again and again with only the indicators of Self-Repair in the open. They can go from the healing process to relapsing to victimization and back again continuously while trying to maintain a balance to recover. The cycle can also keep the body alarms going off repeatedly without their knowing, which is the reason for writing; The Anatomy, Working with Your Body and Basic Brain Science.

A Survivor needs to know what was and is working on their behalf when they cannot seem to find Supportive Agents or Peepers. All humans will have the same internal support but can have different responses in the course of Fight, Flight, or Freeze. They further need to know and understand the Body Agents for themselves. It could be very empowering when a Survivor has right information, while trying to mend the bits, pieces, and parts of Self.

There are Survivors of Trauma and Individuals prone to high stress levels that use methods of Self-Repair. Methods of Self-Repair differ from person to person. The most common of choices are: Drugs, Alcohol, Eating, Withdrawal, and Sleeping etc, though there are host of other methods. Not only are these Self-Repair methods ways of comforting oneself, they can also be indicators of the aftermath. For the most part Self Repair in this manner really has to do with distraction and escaping the life experience. Each method though comforting can become an unhealthy vice to the Survivor. Self-Repair Methods can convert to a ongoing cycle of Obsessive Compulsive Behaviors or Addiction.

S.H.A.D.E.S. hopes to give enough focus with evidence based information concerning Survivors that are prone to lessen their mortality rate. There have been many studies that prove mood disorders, high risk behaviors and addiction are some of the effects of The Childhood Trauma Experiences. Each and every one of the effects mentioned has the ability to further progress into medical problems and legal issues. Studies also confirm that most Survivors have also had ongoing exposure to victimization, re-victimization and trauma left untreated threatening the survival of Survivors.

Maladaptive skills and Self-Repair should be understood as temporal fixes not permanent solution. Body Alarms constantly going off and physiological changes will eventually cause a breakdown of systems. This problem leads to sickness and disease and the possibility of death for several members of a Survivors household. We readily recognize "Family Dysfunction" however untreated trauma and victimization can be a leading cause. We must also keep in mind the Subjective effects in every Survivor. In addition the Survivor must be engaged as a Person that has had an Experience, without converting the Experience to the Person. In other word the Person is more important than the experience. In this way the person isn't treated as secondary to their history.

From 1995-1997 "The Adverse Childhood Experience Study" was conducted by Kaiser Permanente. It's one of the largest investigations into the facts surrounding Childhood Trauma, Abuse, and Neglect with long-term effects. The study continues to be updated and information made available on the Center for Disease Control website. CDC-ACE (Adverse Childhood Experience) shares information on consequences, mortality and morbidity the effects which correlates to the 14 dimensions. Information is good nevertheless power to move-on in the healing process is better therefore, it is encouraged to access the CDC 's website.

Listed on the website are multiple ways to Self-Repair that are deemed as destructive indicators. As with many other studies Substance Abuse is at the top of the list of maladaptive forms of survival techniques that are responsible for household dysfunction. Many studies have been able to group certain Self-Repair techniques into associated groups that include eating disorders, mood changes, anxiety and avoidance. All of which are related to trauma and stress that needs to have an outlet. Its consequences are also validated amongst the mortality and morbidity of a Survivor's adult lifespan. The ACE study proved that the effects of long term childhood trauma experiences are connected to health issues of all kinds.

Many Survivors, especially Young Survivors have been known to remove themselves from a traumatic, painful and violent environment by running away. This might be helpful for them at the moment. Their Self- Repair solution as a runaway can be helpful and harmful at the same time since they are taking the broken, badly bandaged self with them. There has to be more in the way of intervention for the conditions of trauma resolution. Removing self from the environment is only the beginning. There are solutions, though a Runaway may not know where to locate resources or how to access the services. A problem might also arise where the Survivor seeks to protect the Perpetrator. Protecting a perpetrator isn't unusual, many Survivors conceal household violence. They have also been known to protect and conceal their parents or caregivers. Survivors generally don't like repeating or reliving a traumatic episode associated with shame which is a reason for secrecy. And they may also withhold information to what they deem as a shame-based issue.

Survivors are maladaptive to many of their environments and situations that represent harm. However, there's a need for more information and choices to understand how to appropriately service. The S.H.A.D.E.S. Community is symptomatically integrated into multiple Lifestyle-Cultures through Self-Repair and their trauma existence. Another concern is unreported Domestic Violence or Sexual Violence. Many cases have made it clear that without intervention Survivors are prone to victimization and repeated abuse. Whether the victimization or abuse is at the hands of Self or Others are just as important.

NOTES:_____

_____

_____

_____

_____

_____

_____

_____

_____

_____

_____

_____

_____

_____

11 CHAPTER

BRAIN MATTERS

Denial from the S.H.A.D.E.S. perspective heightens our awareness to the fact that it is very possible that a Survivor can be standing in the middle of something. There has been an experience that has them aghast with bits, pieces and parts that has to be put together. In the light of what has happened the Amygdala, the Hippocampus and other body agents have done what is necessary to preserve them. Nevertheless, the Agents are still at work whereas the Amygdala can be in an emergency state. How can this happen?

The Survivor is wounded and living in the primitive state where Self-Preservation Mode has control. Just because Self Preservation has control doesn't necessary mean that the Survivor is aggressive. Though there are aggressive Survivors and there are times when a Survivor is aggressive in some of the 14 dimensions of their life. As with the Author/Writer some Survivors will seemingly return to normal with the long-term memory stored in the Hippocampus. Meaning there is no apparent hindrance Routine Activity which is considered daily living.

Regardless of whether the Survivor is aggressive or not, the Body is in a very aggressive state when in Self-Preservation mode. Therefore, it is necessary to come within the boundaries of S.H.A.D.E.S. to peek at what is going on within the survival state. What the Peeper should ultimately do, is empower the Survivor by educating them on what they have discovered within the boundaries of S.H.A.D.E.S.

Cortisol has been influencing, regulating and modulating several changes in the body in response to overwhelming STRESS. It's a the life sustaining adrenal hormone Body Agent that has protected the Survivor and surrounded the body's homeostasis. Cortisol stops us from feeling emotional and physical pain in order to maintain the focus of survival. The body goes through physiological changes by shutting down systems and overriding others.

In Grays Anatomy is the Cerebral Cortex surfaced in a mass of gyri, sulci and fissures which many of us probably recognizes as bumps, ridges, and wrinkles. However, they are neuron cell bodies across the four hemispheres of the brain. It accounts for at least 80% of the brain where much collaborative activity occurs between the lobes. And although it is a complex Body Agent, its rational, conscious, a big thinker and slower. The reason its slower than other Body Agents is because it's the place where planning, logic, reasoning, and analyzing happens. It's also the most flexible and adaptable to changes that occur through life experiences. When the Emergency Body Agents alarms are set off their controls override the Cerebral Cortex shutting it down.

There are two Body Agents in the brain that store memories, the Cerebral Cortex and the Limbic System. The Body Agents stores two different types of memories, the Cerebral Cortex stores normal memories that are retrievable through associations such as, experience and language. Accessing these memories from the Cerebral Cortex are controllable, connected and integrated. Memories stored in the Cerebral Cortex aren't retrieved with the effects of those stored in the Limbic System. It's one of the differences between experiencing and re-experiencing memories. Trauma memories are stored in the Limbic System, also referred to as our Emotional Brain. Memories at this location are triggered through sensory, stimuli or emotions. Memory retrieval is not controllable, has no language association, and are re-experienced. However, there can be a problem with the memories being dissociate, disconnected or detached as in the, Author/Writers, junction with "What's Beyond the Door?"

It's impossible to talk about trauma without acknowledging the 5 ALARM STRESS RESPONSE that actives all protective mechanisms. The strategic response is more or less equivalent to the Fire Department answering to a 5 alarm fire. Such a fire brings safety divisions full force; First Responders, Fire Department, Police Department, Emergency Medical Services, and Private Ambulatory Services to get safety under control. It would require multiple Engines, Hook and Ladder Companies with Fire Chiefs everywhere such as; with 9/11 though, though 9/11 was more alarming (five five alarm order). Essentially, the Body and its Agents are in a STATE OF EMERGENCY for your safety and preservation.

When talking about trauma it is imperative that we elaborate consciously on TRAUMA related STRESS and the AUTONOMIC NERVOUS SYSTEM (ANS). The Body Agent, that has the actual physiological alterations stored in capacity is the ANS. It's where the Limbic System's Body Agents continues to send signals. And the ANS doesn't know how to stop and re-regulate without supportive assistance from the Survivor. Understanding what happens to the body during and after trauma can help support in re-regulation of the ANS. It's disposition is the result of a stressful state of emergency to the body. And its connected to the Reptilian Brain, which is an unconscious, non verbal and non-cognitive Body Agent. The Body Agent is primitive, not a thinker, it's a reactor that responds without thought or planning when taking action.

We all know the word STRESS, nevertheless we might not know what STRESS is or why it occurs. STRESS is an in-between junction, so to speak. It's a gap between what you want to achieve and what you are able achieve. This particular meaning allows us to know that once again what effects one person might not effect another. Stress can motivate you and promote your growth in different dimensions. It's a healthy and unhealthy element. You can call it, the tension that moves you throughout your day. Stress is a triggering reaction that starts as a feeling and brings about awareness. It effects the whole body as it sends messages to the hypothalamus concerning a threat or overwhelming situation. The hypothalamus sets off an alarm system of nerves and hormones to engage what is perceived as a prevalent attack.

S.H.A.D.E.S. effectively connects us to three major STRESS HORMONES; Adrenaline, Norepinephrine and Cortisol. These take control when we are stressed or in danger and have their own functional purpose.

ADRENALINE also known as Epinephrine, acts immediately and is our Fight and Flight responder. It's a Hormone and a Neurotransmitter.

NOREPINEPHRINE is a neuromodulator that gives a precise evaluation of stressful situations and danger. The main function of Norepinephrine is arousal which in essence is to make one more alert or aware. In a crisis it shifts blood flow to areas of the body, where it's most needed for survival.

CORTISOL is a Steroid Hormone and doesn't act as immediate as Adrenaline or Norepinephrine. It responds simultaneously from a multitask process involving two minor hormones and two Body Agents; the Amygdala and the Hypothalamus. Therefore it takes minutes oppose to seconds to act.

All are involved with the Brain that sends messages to the Adrenal Gland to produce the necessary STRESS HORMONE. Adrenaline and Norepinephrine action are similar in responding. Whereas the Cortisol response can be compared to a Local and Long Distance phone call. Local calls are relevant to Speed Dialing, the push of a button and Long Distance calls uses multiple functions and operators. Let's illustrate the call to the more COMPLEX of STRESS HORMONES.

The Amygdala discerns the threat and sends a message to the Hypothalamus which releases a hormone called, Corticotropin Releasing Hormone (CRH). Then CRH sends a message to the Pituitary Gland to release Adrenocorticotropic Hormone (ACTH). And ACTH sends a message to the Adrenal Gland to produce Cortisol. When Cortisol is released throughout the Body it takes control to preserve life. It influences, regulates and maintains physiological changes in response to STRESS. It responds to Physical and Emotional stress. Cortisol is best known for the activity in the Flight and Fight Response (also known as Flight, Fight or Freeze).

Understand, we all experience Stress daily and it's something that is necessary for our functioning and development. However, too much stress is very unhealthy and can result in medical conditions from the body's constant physiological changes. Therefore, it is important to Manage Stress and Re-regulate the ANS of Trauma Survivors. Otherwise it is a known fact the Body Alarms and Agents will continue a harmful cycle related to Trauma and Distress.

NOTES:_____

_____
_____
_____
_____
_____

12 CHAPTER

DEATH, VICTIMIZATION AND TWISTED REALITIES:

Victimization and Family Dysfunction can be synonymous according to how you view the situations. Knowledge and evidence of the long term Trauma, Neglect, and Abuse effects has made role reversal clear. These are cases where the Childhood Trauma Survivor has become a Perpetrator of some form of violence. There are also cases where Survivors victimize their Loved Ones in the form of Family Dysfunction. It could be as simple as a parent overcompensating a child because of their personal childhood experiences. And in this manner they victimize unknowing and neglect the child. There are parents that have low self-esteem and view the world through their children, making them a target of maltreatment. In most cases if a parent hasn't worked out their childhood trauma issues, chances are they will most diffidently repeat the cycle. Regardless, of how hard they might try not to repeat the past, there will be some form of evidence of neglect or abuse.

Parents and children alike that hold resentment from the past carry toxicity into every relationship. The toxicity might mask itself in family dysfunction and exhibit itself through manifestations of violence. Therefore, the cycle continues without interruption from one Generation to the next. Anyone can become victimized or traumatized through a life experience and suffer long term effects.

Survivors can have overlapping experiences of trauma and victimization and not be aware. From the Author/Writer's testimony its clear to understand that for many trauma begins at home. Whatever memories or experiences of traumatic effects she had, occurred at home. Her reaction to incidents she witnessed at home were far different than those she witnessed in the streets. Furthermore, her reaction to death, danger or threats of violence involving Loved Ones and Close Family Friends always had a tremendous impact on her emotional state.

Death of a Loved One, has been the most traumatizing experience in the Author/ Writer life. It was always something about either the death or the depth of the relationship and sometimes both. As a child her Grandmother passed away and nobody said anything to her about it. For years during certain type of distress she would have a flashback of a childhood memory of her Grandmother.

When she was an adolescent her Mother passed away and it was <u>one</u> of the most tragic experiences of her life. They were very close though her Mother didn't understand the Author/Writers response to certain experiences. One of the things Mother didn't know was she was unable to speak when something shocking occurred. Mother thought in all her frustration she just wasn't answering her. Oh, she could talk sometimes as long as it didn't concern grim details of the experience.

After the death of her Mother, she began to dream dreams of her. In distressing and difficult times she would have flashbacks of particular experiences. Its where trauma and death truly began to change the Author/Writer. She rarely built close relationship because of the impact that came with death. It seemed that in every close relationship, death took its toll. Death became the deterrent for not getting too close to people. The vulnerability that death represented kept her in a place of despair with starting over. Experiences of death also came with victimization during a time of grief which caused an even greater struggle.

When someone has survived any traumatic experience the last thing a Survivor wants to hear is, "you are a victim." Nor do they care to be victimized intentionally or unintentionally. Trauma and death has become synonymous in understanding to the Author/Writer from personal experience.

She had just experience a clash with death and suffer the Loss of "A Loved One." Though her Mother's death tragically changed her, this one was more unusual. This particular death was tragic and defining. There were two prior deaths that she had never shared with anyone and there was a hidden death. The hidden death was angering because it was the death of "A Loved One" and no one notified her. And there was a death that people became desperate about. Now she has six deaths jamming the doors of her life in a way that became unspeakable. The depths of the relationships were of intimate and personal significance. Each death established something other than loss, nevertheless, it was painful, distressing and grievous. And in her despair, in her distress, in her grief she would cling to her Mother last words. After the death of the first two "Loved Ones" it was as though she began to walk in her Mother's last words to her.

Therefore in the wake of the last death of "A Loved One" her distress she was trying as she transitioned. She struggled to stabilize her life and financial stability as she is a Mother, Business Woman and Minister. Her financial struggle shouldn't have be happening and grieved as much damage as Death. There was a unique characteristic involved with this particular extraordinary financial struggle. It was **SITUATIONAL** —An extremely stressful events, causes are man-made in the form of abuse and violence. Someone was purposely orchestrating a series of events that preyed upon a traumatized state. The Author/ Writer also believed that the hidden death of "A Loved One" had a lot to do with what she was experiencing. It was obvious from the tyranny, maliciousness and intrusiveness that someone wanted something. The nature in itself was too cruel to have been the hands of a stranger though the hands of strangers would be used. The hands of stranger were used to cover-up those responsible. Nevertheless, she was aware that the reality of a twisted situation existed. She had spoken out concerning a hidden hand on numerous occasions. And was aware that situational abuse laced in trauma seem to have the actual persons responsible hidden.

She knew she needed help with repeated victimization that existed prior to the Loss of her Loved One. She was having an experience with stalking, harassment and technological theft. Therefore, prior to returning to outside employment she had reported to one of the local agencies that she was being harassed. And was it causing great difficulty in stabilizing her financial well-being. She first sat with a Domestic Violence Specialist who only listened to about 5-minutes of her history. The Specialist told her, you are " A Crime Victim" and gave her a referral to a Crime Unit. Now, the Author/Writer was sure it was a Domestic Violence issue because nobody could get this close except family. Nevertheless, she took the referral across the street to the nearby unit.

Here the Crime Unit Specialist listened to the report concerning; computer hacking, telephone tracking, and other disturbing interruptions to her Independent Professional Life. The circumstances caused financial hardships and was keeping Author/ Writer in an unstable and vulnerable state for assault. She was informed again that she is "A Crime Victim." However, the Victim's Crime Unit didn't seem to have any supporting recommendations for the Author/Writer to return to work. She was only given tips on keeping herself safe during her Routine Activity, such as; "Don't always take the same route when traveling."

Upon leaving the Victim's Crime Unit she could only take deep breaths and say to herself, "okay they have been informed. I have a receipt in the form of a visitors pass that records the date and time. These people aren't listening either. I am a Crime Victim, they said. However, I am also a Victim of Domestic Violence." She knew that the Criminal Assault and Domestic Violence had become intertwined with one over shadowing the other.

The next day she continued to submit online employment application with a bleak outlook. She had been submitting employment application since 2007 to no avail. She had built on an ever changing Independent Professional Career from 2001. She changed phone number multiple times, repaired or replaced her computer multiple times, changed email accounts multiple times, career infrastructure multiple times, etc. Nevertheless, she wouldn't get a response from outside employers. And whenever she was able to use one of her New York State Licenses there would be some type of hostility in the environment. The hostility would be so apparent that is was obvious that someone had infiltrated work environments.

Finally she got a response from an outside employer in the Private Sector and was hired. It didn't take long for Perpetrators to start infiltrating the environment. And those employed to start Self-Supporting in the Criminal Assault. The behaviors were very familiar since she had the same experience in several workplaces and educational institutions. Under the circumstances of what she was experiencing, she reported the activities to "Capable Guardians"(outside of the environment) for the company.

Her co-workers then became more overt and elusively volatile causing work hazards and obstructions. They began to express their discontent at being investigated while Author/Writer monitored their action in order to keep Self out of harm's way. The conditions produced a hostile environment for Author/Writer, Employees, and Patrons. The work environment threatened her Personal and Professional Life.

Emotional, Physiological changes and Self –Repair techniques used to cope were becoming problematic to Self. The hostility created a physiological response when her body alarms were triggered causing Broca's Aphasia. She knew what she wanted to say however, she struggled making the sentence. Her sentences would be either incomplete or start somewhere in the middle of what was to be said. It was for this reason she sought medical attention for anxiety related to Stress during Routine Activities in a hostile environment.

She has already starting using Self Repair Methods that were not beneficial to her stability. Grounding herself at times were more difficult than at other times. Therefore, she learned the procedures and task that she needed to perform and then dissociated from the employees. There were moments during her work shift when she felt as though she was functioning in a three dimensional space. And though she was alert and aware she wasn't in a hyperarousal or hypervigilant state. She had to visit her Primary Care Physical on multiple occasions for assistance with Stress and Anxiety related to the disruptive behaviors in the environment.

Possibly one of the biggest evidence based concerns with Trauma Survivors is victimization. Nevertheless, if Victimization was explored through Trauma Lenses and Victim Precipitation were applied, the insight differs. When dealing with the victimology of an experience, the relationship between victim and perpetrator has a significant part in the findings. The connection between the victim and perpetrator related to social groups and institutions are also key. And it more or less gives indications of possible behaviors of the crime victim that may have contributed to assault. Survivors might become uncomfortable with the information at first. It's not to blame. It's to explore; (1) Victim (2) Perpetrator (3) Lack of a Capable of Guardian relationship. S.H.A.D.E.S. Author/Writer believes it to be important to explore a criminal theory that is applicable to victims of violent crimes such as; Homicide, Robbery, Rape, Assault and Witnessing of Criminal Assault.

Criminologist, Marvin Eugene Wolfgang, preformed an investigative study related to Victim and Perpetrator relationships in collaboration with homicide. Wolfgang's study also concluded that Perpetrators have a chance to become Victims. It's to say that a Perpetrator of an Assault (Motivated Offender) can become the Victim by ways of one of the Theories listed in Victim Precipitation.

VICTIM PRECIPITATION is a concept or theory where the Victim contributes to victimization in some form. Major components are involved in Victim Precipitation; **ACTIVE**--contributes or instigates. **PASSIVE**—unknowingly provokes through aggravation or frustration, which is usually associated with the "assertion of power." **LIFE-STYLE**—influences or increases the likelihood because of low-levels of social control which means life style modification is necessary. **ROUTINE ACTIVITIES**—Daily activities of work and home life can present the triggering behavior. Three elements that must be present when related to Routine Activities; (1) Motivated Offender, (2) Lack of a Capable Guardian, and (3) Suitable Target.

For an individual to suffer a violent assault or witness a horrific incident and then be told they played a part can be re-victimization. Therefore, S.H.A.D.E.S. is going to focus on Routine Activity Theory; using the Author/Writer personal experience: "Death, Victimization and Twisted Realities." When dealing with Victim Precipitation there is an establishment of the relationship between Victim and Perpetrator. However, a Perpetrator essentially might not know the Victim until Motivated Offender comes into place. And in the Author/ Writer's experience the real Perpetrator conducted their affairs as in a Hidden Hand. Which means the Motivated Offender is made visible and in essence became the Perpetrator because of their Motivated Offender position.

ROUTINE ACTIVITIES—Daily activities of work and home life can present the triggering behavior.

- MOTIVATED OFFENDER---a person that is willing when the opportunity is presents, to commit the offense.

- LACK OF A CAPABLE GUARDIAN---forms of security that intervene as a deterrent or obstacles and present a safer environment, such as; police, cameras, well lit areas, etc

- SUITABLE TARGET— a person or property.

If we consider the Victim and Perpetrator coming together through Motivated Offender activity, then we should consider what made the Victim a Suitable Target. We would also have to question the Lack of a Capable Guardian, because we are dealing with Routine Activity.

Under the circumstance of Trauma, Victimization and Twisted Realities, the Author/ Writer experienced extreme stress. Her routine activities became subject to her awareness of a hostile environment. Therefore, she had to devise a strategy to maintain safety and boundaries with the Motivated Offenders. Her strategy cause her to move closer to them in order to monitor their elusive patterns of behavior. She was alert and aware of her surrounding, in addition to having the skills from a professional clinical work history. So, she was already accustomed to monitoring behavioral patterns. What she observed was multiple employees engaged as Motivated Offenders with the Lack of a Capable Guardian simultaneously.

The employees were actively participating in a dangerous cover-up and attempting to whitewash the situation. It wasn't a case of over thinking a situation that was actively engrossing her attention of the environment. Though the environment was equipped with surveillance cameras, which are suppose to be Capable Guardians, it was hostile. And when Capable Guardians outside the environment were informed the Motivated Offenders (Perpetrators) then became victims. Nevertheless, something and someone made the Author/Writer, a Suitable Target.

From the perception of the Author/Writer someone wanted something and this is how they were going about achieving their goal. Because of the extreme financial difficulties and the situational abuse she began to wonder. What did the Perpetrator want? Real Estate difficulties pointed at Real Estate. Family dysfunction pointed at a company she started GLORY INTERNATIONAL AND EMMANUEL. Yet, the computer hacking pointed at the destructive nature that possibly started with the companies. However, after a while the Perpetrators actions began to lurk like a hostile takeover attempt and a deliberate cover-up. These could be the reasoning of the Perpetrator making her a Suitable Target.

If we go back and examine the Passive Concept of victim precipitation the experience has a different angle. The Author/Writer could have very well "Asserted Power" against her a Perpetrator. This could come in the form of speaking out against the perpetrator which is considered, fighting back. It could be calling for justice, or not subjecting or exposing herself to the perpetrator. And in the case of Domestic Violence it could be that she terminated a relationship. When a Survivor asserts power over the perpetrator it is very possible for role reversal to occur. Especially, when the perpetrator exhibits domineering characteristic and becomes provoked through frustration or an inability to have control. In some cases these are the elements that make up the Victim Precipitated Homicide.

NOTES:

13 CHAPTER

LIGHT SHINES OUT OF DARKNESS

S.H.A.D.E.S. have been the surviving agent (Shades Help Adjust Dangerous Experiences for Survivors). The S.H.A.D.E.S. itself is produced by Cortisol. S.H.A.D.E.S. and Cortisol are the relative factors in an emotional, physiological, and a psychological framework of defenses. There are those behind the S.H.A.D.E.S. that have denied the effects of their experience. There are those that blame themselves for their experience. There are those that are in denial about the Survivors experience. And there are those that don't know they are wearing S.H.A.D.E.S.

It can be very difficult for a Survivor to speak up or come to terms with a traumatic experience. However, the physiological effects associated with Flight, Fight or Freeze can be very damaging to the overall health. One thing for sure with trauma is, though, the person may not have recollection of the incident, the body itself remembers. The body has Agents that store memory and the body has Agents that respond to trauma. Psychological maneuvering, silence, a total disconnect from aspects of the experience (be it a person or environment) and disassociating the long-term effects are harmful.

Therefore, we must come to terms with the Substance Cortisol and its many functions. Cortisol belongs to the family of steroid hormones known as glucocorticoids. Glucocorticoid Receptors influence most cells in the our body. It's the receptor that Cortisol and Glucocorticoids bind. Understanding the changes in the body that takes place under cortisol can support a person's health and well-being.

Trauma changes us and our perspective on how we view the world around us over time. Trauma presents our environments and relationships in a perceptive that hadn't been conceived. Depending on the age of the person at the time of the experience there might be an conception of different relationship roles and environments. Nevertheless, after trauma the Mind, Body, and Spirit can be shifted into an altered state. As with the Author/Writer whose existence is immaculate in the freeze response.

Cortisol is a natural stress hormone secreted from the adrenal cortex. It's the active Body Agent in the Flight, Fight or Freeze response. However, cortisol has many functions in the body other than the flight, fight or freeze response. It regulates, influences and modulates many functions within the body. It regulates metabolism and aids in the metabolizing of protein, fat and carbohydrates. It controls the use and levels of sugar, promotes energy through the metabolizing system, and support the immune system. It's involved in the breakdown of glycogen stored in the liver and muscle cells. It helps to reduce inflammation in the body, control blood pressure and salt and water balance. It further has a relationship with our brain that aids with memory formation. Therefore, the many functions of cortisol makes it clear that it promotes our overall health.

Ideally Self Preservation is the primary focus of the cortisol produced S.H.A.D.E.S. Nevertheless, just like anything else we access in life, too much of anything isn't good. Cortisol can shift from our hero to or enemy in the body when chronically elevated and unregulated. The biochemical and stimuli imbalances are the negative flipside to preservation for the Survivor of Trauma. Studies have shown a direct relationships between Childhood Trauma in particular with depression, anxiety, obsessive compulsive behaviors and weight problems. Cortisol has been linked as a risk factor to chronic diseases, and other health problems. The primary link between health problems and diseases is the improper balances and physiological changes in the body.

Just as cortisol aids, supports, and controls various bodily functions, there are Body Agents that control cortisol. Though cortisol is a stress released hormone, the hypothalamus, pituitary gland and adrenal gland controls the activity. Therefore, when it comes to the underlying "Aftermath of Trauma" the problem is with cortisol levels and body alarms. The alarms can be triggered by stress, sensory, stimuli and they can be true, false, and misfiring. Body alarms can become dysfunctional causing the chronic releasing of cortisol resulting in a systematic break down.

High amounts of cortisol interferes with T-Cell creation causing the body vulnerability to pathogen attacks. Which is a clear indicator that cortisol can suppress the immune system. High amounts of cortisol further elevates the blood pressure. Some Survivors use comfort food as a Self-Repair method can develop eating disorders, food addictions, binge, or impulse eating. Often the effects are obesity and unwanted belly fat are related to cortisol levels. The same is demonstrated in Substance Abuser with a common thread of Childhood Trauma and comorbidities. The common thread or underlying issue promotes unsafe behaviors that may be connected to Self Repair mechanisms that fail.

The body is not intended to function in a chronic state of emergency with Body Agents administering a chain reaction that includes overriding systems. Which causes all systems except those needed for the immediate survival to control physiological changes. A cascade of hormones are released, blood is increased 300% by diverting from areas not imperative to survival. Some systems are shut off and blood and oxygen are sent to muscles, brain, lungs and heart. And to make matters worse when the threat has passed the reaction is suppressed in the

ANS. The chronic malfunction is that of a physiological roller-coaster ride abusing the body and its systems.

Therefore, when examining the effects of harmful cortisol levels it's imperative to know and understand that STRESS is the major component. It's what has kept something ajar in the life of the Survivor. Stress, a necessary element of the body can be the hardest to control in various circumstances.

From the perspective that Light Shines Out Of Darkness the light comes from the knowledge and understanding that can guide. Family Dysfunction and Health Morbidity are the two roots connected to the damage of a Traumatic History. All three ultimately effect the Mortality rate of individuals, families, communities, and social groups with co-occurring effects that can be prevented and limited, instead of promoted. In addition all three are active participates in some form of violence. The violence can be physical, personal, professional, environmental, or within the internals and externals of the body.

Today more and more Professionals and Non Professional are using techniques to address the influx of violence, family dysfunction, and trauma. Not all Survivors are receptive to the interventions and preventive measures. Some are going to take offense to what they correlate to a shame-based issue as stated previously. And what they need to understand is they're relationship is toxic to individuals, families, communities and social groups. Though some surviving members of the community are going to respond to breaking a cycle of death and darkness.

From a S.H.A.D.E.S. perspective if we examined the development of traumatic effects cortisol and self repair our subject illuminates. Example: Trauma happens, Survivor uses

Alcohol/Drugs to Self Repair, altered states become addictive and causes risky lifestyle. Lifestyle engagement provokes compromising chronic diseases and other health issues. Family and Communities are effected via quality of life of a Survivor in an altered state of existence. Mortality effects can be influenced by Domestic Violence, Victimization, H.I.V. Diabetes, Cardiovascular problems and other forms of morbidities are in the shadows. The shadows are next in line for at-risk effects from the traumatic history with cortisol and stress.

NOTES:_____

_____

_____

_____

_____

_____

_____

_____

_____

_____

_____

_____

14 CHAPTER

SHIFT AND FLOW

S.H.A.D.E.S. perspective belief is that Trauma should be approached in a three-fold manner in order to support the Survivor. (1) The Trauma Itself, (2) The Physiological and Emotional Changes, and (3) Re-regulation of the body and Release of Trauma. Sometimes it not a matter of Re-experiencing the Trauma as much as putting the pieces of Self back together.

Earlier in S.H.A.D.ES. we mentioned that Survivors have a tremendous amount of wealth that is comparison to "The Euphrates River" however there must be a breach for the waters to flow. S.H.A.D.E.S has covered much of a three-fold approach; (1) Trauma, (2) Physiological and Emotional (The Body Agents), now we are entering the third-fold. This is where we integrate some of the information, Re-regulate the Body and Release the Trauma. And it could be the hardest part because it also deals with the desire to Self Repair. For this reason the last few chapters 15-26, of the S.H.A.D.E.S. educational manual contains Relapse Prevention, Self Soothing and Relaxation Techniques.

Some might wonder why there is a chapter on Human Potential however this is an acceptable concept of dimension recognized in the field of Trauma. S.H.A.D.E.S. elaborates more on dimensions individually as they function collectively. Well-known expert and speaker Olga Phoenix engages topics on Trauma recognizes dimensions. According to Olga Phoenix who is a Master of Public Administration (MPA) and Master of Art (MA) there are at least Six-

Dimensions that we all share; (1) Physical (2) Psychological (3) Emotional

(4) Spiritual (5) Personal and (6) Professional.

Olga Phoenix works confirms what Author/Writer of S.H.A.D.E.S. have been saying for years through her Sole-Proprietor Company "EMMANUAL." In order for a person to function to their greatest of potential you must work to maintain a Personal and Professional balance. You cannot neglect the Personal and support the Professional or vice-versa without becoming unhealthy in both areas. Olga Phoenix states the Six-Dimensions function as One and S.H.A.D.E.S. denotes that 14- Dimensions function collaboratively and some balance other areas. Its especially true when 14 or 6 dimensions are divided into the 3 aspects of Body, Mind, and Spirit. Though one dimension can balance other dimensions, Personal and Professional Development is the motivating factor. It can be tough for some Survivors, however the person has to make an effort to foster a nurturing relationship with Self in order to support and focus on their development.

Many Survivors, mature through Personal storms to pursue a passionate career. Whether it's an Independent Professional Industry or Public/ Private Sector, Survivors find their place in the world. And some develop a passion of creativity focused on helping other people. Many forge a union with spiritual wellness to support their development through life's personal storms. Trauma can change a person's perspective of how they view the world, nevertheless, the healing process changes their perspective as well. The healing process can bring about rest and release of distress and enables one to move on to a better position in life. Some begin to seek out their purpose for living and positive fulfillment in this life. Because there is life after trauma and a Survivor should know how to survive outside the negative impact of trauma.

The Author/Writer worked and struggled to maintain Professional Development as she overcame storms in her Personal Development. She went from establishing several Businesses to becoming a Peer Educator, Credentialed Alcohol and Substance Abuse Counselor Trainee and Recovery and Life Coach. Her counseling education training includes; Childhood Trauma Education, Women, Substance Abuse and Post-traumatic Stress Disorder to name a few. She further developed in more competitive and Independent Professional Industries; Property Management, Building Maintenance Technician, Real Estate, Property and Casualty Insurance, and Notary. If not all but most of her professional engagements are New York State Licensed or Certification required. Her other trainings and education are for personal and professional knowledge that supports her career goals. Achievement should be encouraging for Survivors that have doubts concerning life after Childhood Trauma and other Traumatic Experiences. It is always best to draw from strengths that shall strengthen their weakness.

The professional industries from which the Author/Writer indentifies represents two different worlds. These realms coexist with different perceptions. Though both professional realms are laced with protocol, the real property world is more organized than the people skills world. The Author/Writer has a preference to the Private Sector and has worked in Government through a contract from the Private Sector. She has found that the Private Sector offers more leverage for upward mobility. And she has always focused on her Personal Life not getting in the way of her Professional Life.

For decades S.H.A.D.E.S. Author/Writer struggled with the effects of Trauma Experiences and Self-Repair as she sought to move on Personally and Professionally. She fostered a union with her Spiritual belief system and models of Clinical Professionals such as; Judith Herman (Trauma and Recovery), James W. Pennebaker (Writing to Heal), Lisa M. Najavitis (Seeking

Safety) Ellen Bass and Laura Davis (The Courage to Heal). Strangely enough she also found support from; Mike Lew (Victims No Longer), Daniel Jay Sonkin (Wounded Boys Heroic Men), Patrick A. Means (Men Secret Wars) and multiple local Crisis Professionals. Each Clinician mentioned gave her personally what she needed, when it was needed (empowering knowledge) aiding in the grasping of the effects related to processing trauma.

Margaret Vasquez an Independently Licensed Professional Counselor, Certified Trauma Therapist, and Certified Intensive Trauma Therapy Instructor impacted S.H.A.D.E.S., Author/ Writer through "The Instinctual Trauma Model Explained." Before going into this segment the words Instinctive and Instinctual must be define.

Instinctive according to science describes an unlearned response regardless of how basic such as the flight, fight, or freeze response. Whereas instinctual describes feelings, thoughts, behaviors, deep associated tendencies and motivation. On the opposite spectrum without scientific input instinctive is literal and instinctual is figurative. The Author/ Writer makes the distinction through her relationship with The Experience, Trauma and Expression via which she writes.

Therefore, when Margaret Vasquez "Explained the Instinctual Response Trauma Model" more things began to make sense behind the Author/ Writer's, S.H.A.D.E.S. Margaret Vasquez simply explained how Trauma effects the Brain. The left hemisphere of the Brain which some refer to as the left brain is responsible for; verbal, math, logic, problem solving, linear, sequential. The left hemisphere is systematic, strategic planner and subject to rational thinking and behavior. The Author/ Writer of S.H.A.D.E.S. refers to the Left Brain as the Rational Mind. The right hemisphere of the Brain which some refer to as the right brain is responsible for; nonverbal, creativity, holistic, artistic, musical, disconnected-bits and pieces, gut feeling, intuition, emotional. The right hemisphere is causal free in its thinking and behavior. The Author/ Writer of S.H.A.D.E.S. refers to the Right Brain as the Mind of Passion.

The left and right hemisphere coexist in their separate mental realms with the equivalent of two worlds. What makes the hemispheres emulate two apparent mental worlds? The Left hemisphere "Seat of Reason" and Right hemisphere "Seat of Passion." The dynamics differ in organization and expressive language. The corpus callosum connects the left and right hemisphere and <u>under normal circumstances</u> most people function using both hemispheres. However, Stress hormones related to trauma constricts the left hemisphere and causes the trauma to be encoded in the right hemisphere.

The Right Hemisphere, the nonverbal and unconscious Body Agent, is interconnected to the Limbic System. Though the Right Hemisphere is nonverbal its very expressive. It reads facial expressions and body language. It emotionally expresses and in secret stores the trauma memories. When factoring in denial and dissociation (unawareness) it's because the Right Hemisphere has hidden the trauma. The encoded memories doesn't mean that the Survivors don't remember the incident. However, there are cases in which Survivors have trauma related Amnesia. The Right Hemisphere also keeps the Left Hemisphere which assist in Routine Activities from being overwhelmed with intrusive trauma thoughts.

Therefore, with the Instinctual Trauma Response Model recovery begins with the Right Hemisphere which is very active in comparison to the Left Hemisphere. The Author/Writer in a death related, grief stricken and traumatized state continued to shift and flow in her Personal and Professional life. She would go from the Rational Mind to the Mind of Passion and express herself in both realms. Her memories containing "Death of Loved Ones" were always in a state of "Now" though she was aware it was the past. The Left and Right Hemisphere experiences time differently. The Left experiences past, present, and future and the Right only the now making it emotionally the present. Because her memories always presented as "Now" they were always fresh. She was able to push them into yesterday because she knew it wasn't "Now" the deaths had already past. Yesterday was as far back as she could push them because of the depth of the emotions, a lack of closure, and victimization.

There has been research that has established that the "Seat of Passion" (Right Hemisphere) dominates Social and Emotional functions over the "Seat of Reason" (Left Hemisphere). It's very active and engaging with emotional dominance that expands bilaterally to the Autonomic Nervous System (ANS) and in an upset state, physiological changes occur. The "Seat of Passion" expressed the instinctual describing her feelings, thoughts, behaviors, deep associated tendencies and motivation.

Death distressed the Author/Writer to the point of despondency and emotional despair. The grief would immobilize her into a state of numbness where she felt separated from the world and people around her. Death presented with a perception of having control over life situations making her powerless. The experience would often cause her to be emotionally stuck without a way of expressing what she was feeling. She would attempt to come to term with "Blessed are those who Mourn."

Grief a perplexing intense sorrow associated with Brokenheartedness caused by the loss of "A Loved One" She had become acquainted with Grief and things that has caused a great unhappiness in life. Her Grief has many layers of emotions connected to the sorrows, gaps in coherence of the happening, and fragmentation of Life. Yet, S.H.A.D.E.S. are blocking the intensity of this pain associated with grief. Not only is there sorrow, there is Anger, Denial, Fear, Lack of Trust and multiple matters that all pertains to the brokenheartedness and feelings of Betrayal.

Nevertheless, she would attempt to exit the shocking state and it was to no avail because of her understanding of Death. She had become to know Death through Spirit and Personhood which made each experience different and difficult. She took Death's behaviors personal and she thought Death to be rude. She believed that Death had no boundaries for which it respected people. She didn't care much for its personal attributes and had to come through Professional Logos to understand Death's perspective on life. She had an idea that Death had his argument, statement, and principle reason, nevertheless he is hard to grasp. And she clearly didn't understand his reasoning of why.

Therefore, it is through Personal and Professional Development she learn to "Shift and Flow." She created paradigm shifts through **PHYSICAL, SPIRITUAL, EMOTIONAL, ENVIRONMENTAL, CREATIVE,** and **IMAGINATIVE** dimensions. **PHYSICAL, SPIRITUAL, EMOTIONAL** and **ENVIRONMENTAL** habitats are where most human exposure is experienced. And for expressing and grounding her experience with Death and other trauma she engaged **CREATIVE** and **IMAGINATIVE** dimensions. Shift and Flow coordinated how she expressed her trauma, dissociation, lack of closure, and victimization. Using creative and imaginative dimensions she began to express her pain Instinctually. The "Seat of Passion" released the trauma often using the figurative when expressing what she was feeling and wanted to say and couldn't. Nevertheless, from the "Seat of Passion" she began to flow like a river which supported a ship of jewels and other material wealth.

JOVAN~KA CONYERS....S.H.A.D.E.S.

She separated herself from situations and clarified others through identification. A prime example would be how she identifies in S.H.A.D.E.S. as Author/ Writer. Though the identifying terms (Author/ Writer) might seem interchangeable to some, the meanings differ. An Author creates the thought, design, or contents of the work being written. While the Writer is the person who writes the literary work. However, the Author/ Writer can be one and the same such as in the works of S.H.A.D.E.S.

Writing, the most empowering activity she engaged would breach her Euphrates making waves for what she couldn't verbally express. During times of extreme stress and trauma related storms, she was unable to speak. Nevertheless, she could write what she felt, knew, and thought. Writing subdued her inability to verbalize and created a way to shift and flow. She began to write journals, poetry, books, proposal, business plans and documented dreams and visions. She documented fragmented dreams that she didn't understand, however, she knew they had some type of meaning, whether past, present, or future.

The "Seat of Passion" had authority over her traumatic experiences and she began to write intimately. The "Seat of Reason" kept things organized and between the "Two Seats" she maneuvered during Routine Activities. Instinctively she was aware of Stress response. Instinctually she used writing to describe her intimate feeling and thoughts concerning behaviors. Since the traumatic experiences were connected to relationships that held significance she wrote her unspoken words literally and figuratively. Most often what was literal came forth figuratively. However, because of deep associations there had to be some type of identification to ground the experience.

The Author/Writer published a book called BRAGGADOCIO she wrote using the "Seat of Passion" to describe a traumatic experience of Criminal Assault and Victimization. Her 9/11 experience might seem awkwardly written, however, it was a matter of the "Seat of Reason" organizing for the "Seat of Passion." Therefore there is a separation and distinction between relationships and titles of people. Though 9/11 was a traumatic experience there were those within her midst that had troubled her unnecessarily. Grounding herself through identifying various aspects of experiences became a matter of Nouns, Verbs, Adjectives etc. It was like speaking another language that could be well understood through the dimension of Creativity and Imagination.

The Author/Writer's, Routine Activities were everything except Routine Activities. They were traumatic and violent for the most part. Her Routine Activities exposed the behaviors, morals, values of people around her, whether Personal or Professional. The Lack of a Capable Guardian, Stalking and Criminal Activity constantly posed a threat, hindering "Trauma Recovery." She experienced times when she was literally forced out of employment or undermined. There was a pattern that could clearly be identified with FINANCIAL ABUSE causing wreckage.

Independently as a Professional she appeared to be scattered about or long-gated because someone was tracking and trying to control her livelihood. Whoever is responsible is someone she either broke ties with or simply wanted what she owned. She maneuvered away from many of her Rights as a Person to the degree that circumstances could be easily identify with Human Rights Violations. She was adamant in keeping her distance from what and who she deemed as the enemies to her house.

Via using Victim Precipitation she was able to ground and maintain her balance against the hidden hand. There is no other terminology or dynamics that could describe a "Vicious Attack" other than the words of a Survivor. The Perpetrator was worse than Death from every apparent aspect. Always seeking to control or destroy and moving through Motivated Offenders. The pattern had all the dynamics of Situational Abuse which is always man-made to cause harm that could result in trauma.

She knew the possibilities of breaching her grief and causing a flow within the dimensions. She would have to shift, what she "could not" changed. Although some things couldn't be changed other things could be stopped with Capable Guardians. Therefore, she shifted creatively and imaginatively breaching the walls of the Euphrates causing a flow of Professional productivity. She was constantly reframing some of her experiences which became one of her greatest of assets.

The "Seat of Reason" and the "Seat of Passion" which are two separate mental states enabled her to endure Routine Activities. And though she was able to endure she was never accepting of the disruptive Routine Activity behaviors.

The toughest part would be getting the ANS under control that continued to respond to sensory and stress stimuli. There would be times when she would become upset and it would take her three days to a week to calm down. She would use a variety of tools; Self Repair, Relaxation Techniques and sometimes she had to get medical assistance. During these times she continued her Routine Activities as though unaffected. However, she was very much affected by the Motivated Offenders and Perpetrators unwanted activities.

The ANS Body Agent responding internally to extreme stress and stimuli can physically alter creating sickness, disease and chaos. From the external, the body can alter relationships in social dimensions and cause dysfunction as in family. For the most part trauma related family dysfunction is more in tuned with Self Repair that motivates a Survivor to escape. Self

Repair is a maladaptive skill or escape mode that can have long-term harmful effects without intervention.

The Author/Writer has had tremendous struggles with Self Repair. As her memory recollect when being assessed for trauma the questions were always related to sexual and physical abuse as a child. And no clinician had ever asked had she experienced any significant deaths as a child or an adult. However, Death and Grief are major parts of why she wears S.H.A.D.E.S. Some things are synonymous as previously said. You can have Grief without Trauma, nevertheless, You cannot have Trauma without Grief. And for some Death represents both Trauma and Grief, which is the Author/Writer's case. Death and Trauma both represent a loss that can only be determined in significance by the Survivor.

NOTES:_____
_____
_____
_____
_____
_____
_____
_____
_____
_____

15 CHAPTER

WE LIFT OUR HEAD IN THE SANCTUARY:

There should be a place that is "A Personal Safe Place" called a "Sanctuary." For many people a place of Worship or Church might come to Mind but the place doesn't have to be either. S.H.A.D.E.S. centers the Sanctuary in the environmental surrounding; a place of refuge or protection, a place of justice immune from abuse or harm. Home environments can be laden or laced with extremely restraining and restrictive laws, posing as rules. The sanctuary is a place that is Holy and Sacred within where you are protected.

From the definition and understanding of the above a Sanctuary is a place of refuge or a shelter from harm. It is "A SAFE SPACE" that you are to call your own. The Sanctuary has inner and outer walls. It has walls that are visible and walls that are invisible. It's a Personal Space. There are "BOUNDARIES" in the Sanctuary in other words lines that you can't violate, trespass on, or cross. Because it is a place where you are to be free from harm and can be freed from pain. Emotional Stressors are painful, quite often many are open wounds, and many are unable to see the scars but in the Sanctuary they are cleansed and healed.

A Sanctuary is something you can create that has inner and outer walls of protection. But first you have to set up boundaries that protect "You" from Self and Others in order to have PERSONAL SAFE SPACE for starters. When in the Sanctuary you are able to Release the Stress of the Pain, Trouble, Grief, and Anger that tied you to Fear and Denial. In order to have the Sanctuary you have to make the decision to build the inner and outer wall. And install protective statutes "You" have to establish the BOUNDARIES on the FOUNDATION OF

SAFETY.

In Establishing your plans you have to measure the surroundings and evaluate the sustainability by making an assessment of the possible Safety, Harm, and Limit the Amount of Danger (*S.H.A.D.E.S.).* There are things, events, and occurrences that many Cultures and Traditions forbid to be acknowledged even if they have hurt somebody. However, this is Your Sanctuary that is outside that which has been established and has caused "You Pain." Your S.H.A.D.E.S. are tinted, darkened, dimmed, shaped and molded and fostered in the view that stumbles you.

Measurements of the limits between; You, Yourself, and Others should be a starting point. This is where you draw the line as to how close you permit Others to come in YOUR Sanctuary. In measuring the limit on the space you will allow for Yourself, you should evaluate what you are comfortable with opening Yourself too. S.H.A.D.E.S. has kept you in a place where you really have a degree of separation from "Yourself". The separation may have caused emotional complications with others. And when it comes to "You" it's best if you start with what makes "You" comfortable enough to sit with "Yourself".

Something as simple as designating an area and some time to the area where you would consider building YOUR SANCTUARY promotes safety. Then clear, clean, decorate the walls, floors and consider the type of furniture. You could choice some assortment of "Personal" things from flowers, music, books, pictures that make you happy and light that is always there when you decide to go into the Sanctuary at a time you hadn't planned. Don't forget a mirror to watch you grow. It is always good to surround "Yourself" with the Beauty that "You" are.

This area may cause you to look over your life as you have known it from behind the

S.H.A.D.E.S. There may be happy memories and some not so happy. Take your Journal with you into this area. If something is too painful, just take it a little at a time because the choice is up to you how much and what you want to open from a painful past. The pain could be the loss of a loved one, pain someone caused you, or some other occurrence that has made you hide yourself from yourself. There may be tears, laughter, and question that need answers that you just don't understand. So, don't forget the tissue and remember its okay to cry to wash away the pain.

There are going to other Emotions that surface such as; Anger, grief, anxiety, fear and of cause denial. As you go through there will also be a Residue of Emotions that will surface with its connectedness. Therefore, give "Yourself" Time and Space. All of these Emotions will surface with some degree of Stress and you really don't have to go through by yourself. Just as you have to limit Others, remember it's possible you may have to do this with Self. However, limitations are the most important contribution to your Sanctuary. The BOUNDARIES are all about LIMITS.

RESPECT FOR BOUNDARIES:

As previously stated BOUNDARIES are for "Your protection and separates "Your Personal Space from Others. Healthy Boundaries limit the space to keep you from suffering from unnecessary emotional distresses and pain. It supports your mental, physical, emotional and spiritual dimensions of your human composition. The boundaries' stops your environmental space against pollutants from Toxic Relationships. Establishing boundaries builds on many grounds that support; Your Self Esteem, Emotional Health, Gives you control, builds Trust, and Secures you in Creating Loving relationships with Self and Others.

Many will have to assess Toxic Relationships amongst; Family, Friends, and Community. All three of these particular relationships have the ability to cause you to Neglect yourself and what you truly desire. Immediate family members have a way of being manipulative, cunning, and masterminding some of the violence in your life. Your Parents may have set up unhealthy system of enmeshed that may cause you to believe that you are obligated to your Siblings and connected you to relationships in ways that you are really not. You may have a relationship with friends that you believe are as close too, you as a Brother or Sibling. However there is a possibility that they contribute to the same Toxic Relationships as family. Then there's the community that may be acquainted with your Lifestyle and Culture that must be assessed as time change, people change, and community changes. Sometimes communities don't know the difference between holding hands and chaining souls therefore you should.

You must further be honest enough to honor "Yourself" which is the True Self in hiding for lack of boundaries in your life where those around you have; trespassed, violated, and jeopardized your personal safety. People Pleasers are well aware of the pain that they feel when they have dishonored themselves for another. In the Sanctuary you begin to distinguish love from hate, trust from betrayal, and who you are from who you think you are. You are not obligated to deny you have been hurt to yourself for the sake of an argument or to receive love, affection, and attention from negative people or toxic relationships. Boundaries will help you break these ties and limit the access and involvement with these persons related to their pain involved in your life.

Healthy Boundaries must have flexibility and adaptability without Your Safe Space and Safe Space of Others being violated. Just as you establish boundaries that you want respected you also have to respect the boundaries of others. There are basic needs such as food, clothes and shelter which are simplest essentials of human need and personal space. Then there are the more complicated haves such as money, property, and the ability to provide for others that can become very complex when you are dealing with people who believe without merit they have entitlement. Meaning they have the right to share in your stuff whatever it is and they actually don't have that right.

EFFECTIVE COMMUNICATION helps you establish and maintain the boundaries and that are needed. You have to express what it is you want, need and don't want or need. Boundaries are stable with effective communication and standing your ground with fairness, privacy and protection. Boundaries are easily breached when outsiders don't know where they stop and where you begin. Underestimating your personal space is as bad as a player reaching in during a game of basketball. The Referee signals a foul in the game because the rules, perimeters and structure of the fair game have been violated. Often without the Referee blowing his whistle, calling the play, and stopping the interference, violence is possible to erupt the game and environment. The Safe Space of the basketball court as well as the area that is surrounded with sports fans is violated.

HEALTHY COMMUNICATION:

In order to have healthy communications you have to be clear, on your wants and need once again. While building the SANCTUARY, establishing BOUNDARIES, and making your POINT you have INNER PEACE. Remember that's why the walls are there it's not for the sake of avoiding a conflict or conversation. There are inner walls and outer walls to the Personal Self and to the Environment. S.H.A.D.E.S. is big on "EXPRESS YOURSELF" it takes into account your Emotions, Experiences, and Honors who you are inside and outside. The Sanctuary is also protected inside and outside because of the established boundaries.

Learning to "LIVE YOUR LIFE" after years of abuse, hurt, emotional turmoil, and holding on to grief that should be mourned and expressed; COMMUNICATION is the next step. Therefore, we must start the assessment of the People who shut your life off in a way that S.H.A.D.E.S. has been your lengthy support. The S.H.A.D.E.S. has been changing shapes, tints, and growing progressively darker as the days go by under denial. For clarity Denial is basically a defense mechanism for an occurrence that you cannot accept at a particular moment in your life. So, breakout your Journal, get the pen that has power and jot their names down to stop the chaos. This will help you in tearing through the rubbish that has kept you buried in silence. One of the things you should know is Silence means death to your inner being. One more thing, don't forget to put your name on the list only because you could have trapped parts of you. Don't worry about feeling guilty for now S.H.A.D.E.S. is taking you to GLORY. You will ultimately and eventually move from glory to glory in your transition.

It's time to take down the Names and Numbers and you can put your name any where you honestly feel safe. The Names and Numbers can change position as you feel you need them and in the order you need. You simply screen these Names and Numbers using four steps of identification. (1) What did you witness/ experience? (2) What did you think? (3) What did you feel? (4) What do you need? There is something to be said about what you experienced, thought, felt and needed. Though we need discipline in our lives unexpected hurt, pain, assaults, abuse and pinned up emotions is not what we need or wanted from those you believed are loving members of your environment. Please don't try to do all this in a day because stress, mourning, and anger could erupt at various times. And you still have to be able to function throughout developmental stages.

Building a relationship with Self will make life more enlightening as you take the steps necessary to engage others. Communication builds healthy relationships because we are relational, social, and intellectual humans that can only develop self and others through healthy effective communication. For clarification, in sharing yourself with yourself and others be mindful who you share what with. There are people that have a tendency to victimize others with Self Disclosure. That's the reason for using the Journal to protect your boundaries and privacy until you are ready to share with anyone else. It will also help you to address your emotional stress without hurting Self and Others. Using the Journal is an acceptable way of removing some of the inner toxicity. However, it is not Self Disclosure there has to be someone engaging the information you share to be Self Disclosure.

One of the best techniques you could learn is "ASSERTIVENESS SKILLS" a social behavior that is grasped overtime. It doesn't require you to be "Aggressive" only that you express your thoughts, feeling, the needs you desire and stand up for your RIGHTS. There are times when you use AGGRESSION to protect your LIFE and PROPERTY. Through "Assertiveness" you open the door to healthy relationships, communication and maintain your boundaries. Knowing your Rights taps into various areas of your Life and Relationships. Culture, Tradition and perceived Family Trust could be only equated with Betrayal and contradict your Rights to Express Yourself.

- ♠ You have the Right to Speak for yourself and put yourself first at times.
- ♠ You have the Right to Say No when you really want to say No; not yes
- ♠ You are human and have the Right to err
- ♠ You have the Right to step against criticism
- ♠ You have the Right to Change your mind

- ♠ You have the Right to express your opinions and stand in your convictions
- ♠ You have the Right to intervene on behalf of Self to clarify what you mean
- ♠ You have the Right to Social, Emotional, and Spiritual, support and ask for Help
- ♠ You have the Right to choose
- ♠ You have the Right to feel and express your pain

These are some of the Rights you have and need to know when it comes to your welfare and security. Though there are times you will hear things and not like the Criticism but be clear there is Constructive Criticism. These are times it's in your best interest to Listen. Probe what's being said and then acknowledge what's for you and what's not. Constructive Criticism is for the purpose of Improvement. If you Reflect on why one uses a COACH as in why someone acknowledges S.H.A.D.E.S. It's only for sharpening your abilities for Personal or Professional growth. There will be conflict within your life and attitudes that you can't change in other people only in yourself. Learning to NEGOTIATION and how to FIGHT FAIR, which IS healthy in communicating your needs and fostering relationships without breaching boundaries.

NEGOTIATION:

Knowing how to come to a mutual understanding or reasonably resolving a conflict entails that communication be set within boundaries. However, before you start wrestling with what you cannot change understand there will be relationships are known as irreconcilable differences. And you don't have to be ashamed or feel guilty for acknowledging you must let go. Many people behind S.H.A.D.E.S. probably don't like conflict and possibly are fearful of conflict because they see it as confrontation. They view confrontation within a relation to hostility in the eyes of violence, aggression, and problematic due to their experience. But to have healthy boundaries and to express yourself there must be effective communication. It takes courage to speak from behind S.H.A.D.E.S., to a perceived threat to your emotions, mental state, and physical health.

Your experience is valid, the pain, and the fear is real. Nevertheless, in order to develop a healthy form of communication it takes SKILLS. And what are skills? It's an Art, a know-how, a creative way of doing something. In priming the skill it takes a frame of work and a method with a mindset that promotes your abilities. There are usually principles involved that are guidelines which are really boundaries of effectiveness. Negotiation is a way of reaching an agreement where as confrontation is relative to face or oppose boldly, defiantly, or something that competes as an adversary.

Conflict on the other hand is an everyday part of life that must be proactively processed in resolution. There are some differences between FAIR FIGHTING and UNFAIR FIGHTING. Both have opposing components that illustrate the healthy and unhealthy in other words' fairness and unfairness. Unfairness is a combination of blame, anger as the dominating emotion; inconvenient time, unreasonable damages, laying everything on out on the table all motivating pain and stress with no productive outcome. Whereas, fairness is a combination of organizing in preparation to work out the problems using; a set time, outlining issues, addressing one issue at a time, not casting blame, taking responsibility for actions, and working out reasonable solutions that motivate change. Here we can see the clear difference between the unproductive and the productive in comparison to fair fighting and unfair fighting. And putting things plainly Fair Fighting is Constructive as in building bridges and Unfair Fighting is Destructive as in blowing up bridges.

People wearing S.H.A.D.E.S. often come from relationships where trust is broken, abuses exist, and grief became unbearable. In all these are very Emotionally Stressful situations especially in combination with "The loss of a Loved One or Betrayal in Loved One." It leaves to question then with all this Emotional Stress and Pain behind the S.H.A.D.E.S. How do we handle conflict? Well, S.H.A.D.E.S. helps adjust dangerous experiences for Survivors. These experiences contain issues with denial, stress, fear, anxiety and anger. So, now we reframe some of the STRESS, which is more powerful, then the anger, fear and denial. This changes the environmental outlook and restructures for Expressing Yourself. One or two of the simplest examples, are the format of a meeting with a Counselor or a Business meeting where one usually expects a positive outcome to some degree.

WE NEED TO TALK:

Whenever these forms are set up there is always a Structure even in an emergency therefore, a time is set, the problems are laid out, issues are separated in the problem not the person. The goal is to come to a mutual understanding. Terms of interest and reasonable efforts are made on everybody's behalf. Sometime you have to agree to disagree because we don't always agree but some things can be achieved without compromising one's integrity, belief, or rights. There may be some EMOTIONAL EXCITEMENT without hostility and anger dominating the structure. There should be no hidden agendas or undermining of another or threatening body language. We can use the terms of a legally binding contract where fairness, commitment and mutual terms exist regardless of the signature.

In order for a legally binding contract to exist there must be fairness to all parties involve. (1) Competent parties (2) age–meaning maturity (3) mutual agreement (4) reasonable

(5) without duress. All these can bring you through healthy negotiations with a commitment towards change. Avoidance is never the key to resolving conflict because with neglect there are consequences that will affect various areas of your Life.

REMEMBER: The fundamental of the healthy skills are incorporated and primed over time for EFFECTIVE COMMUNICATION to EXPRESS YOURSELF from behind the S.H.A.D.E.S. All the information we covered should help you secure YOUR SAFE SPACE. Now, what have you assessed, evaluated, and established?

Write in a Journal what you extracted from the empowering information. Write what techniques you can use, have experience with and must be applicable to your life as you understand. Prior moving on to the next chapter you should review what you have obtained in the Sanctuary. Try to use any of the techniques related to boundaries and healthy communication. S.H.A.D.E.S. encourages you to maintain your protection, privacy, and learn that LIFE IS A PROCESS. This is the main reason for the JOURNAL because what is written pertains to your Personal Space. And you don't have to share any ANGUISH OR PAIN that you feel until you are ready. As we journey on, you will discover the various PROCESSES, STAGES, and TRANSITIONS you will go through. In the process S.H.A.D.E.S. changes TINTS, SHAPES, and LENSES.

A BREATH OF FRESH AIR:

The Sanctuary should be as a breath of fresh air in order to help you engage in being comfortable with yourself. When building your PERSONAL SAFE SPACE that creates BOUNDARIES in order to reduce your stress. Though as time goes on, your time outs will increase awareness and alert you to stress related activities and unsafe space.

Therefore take the time to learn these simple steps whether sitting or standing. Proper standing requires you position your feet firmly with them slightly spread apart. Raising your arms as you inhale and lower them as you exhale can help breath monitoring. Proper sitting requires a comfortable chair, upright position, feet are to be firmly planted or crossed whichever you choose. Lowering your head to your chest as you inhale and raising it when you exhaling can help you with the monitoring of breathing. Keeping count of your breath during the technique can also be helpful.

These techniques can be done in as little as 60 seconds to 3 minutes of your time. You must be conscious of listening to your breath and start by taking short breaths. Paying attention to the listening portion of the exercise will cause you to take deeper breath from the abdomen. There can be an experience of a euphoric that comes from the breath being infused during the exercise. You must be consistent in order to maintain your balance related to stress and anxieties that might be companions.

Breathing has enormous effect on the body as it releases pinned up energy, releases toxins, promotes self-esteem, releases a BODY AGENT called ENDORPHINS. Which supports natural tranquility, reduces stress, rejuvenates strength, reduces harmful cravings and blood sugar, increase blood circulation and oxygen to cells and tissues. These are just of few benefits of the Breathing Techniques that also aides the immune system and essentially don't cost you a red penny. It only takes time and commitment to your personal care that does the body good with the internal and external struggles of environments.

NOTES:_____

_____

16 CHAPTER

WATCHING YOUR STEP

We've taken several steps in the education of the possible reasons and experiences of the Person behind the S.H.A.D.E.S. Applying new techniques takes practice, maintaining balance and reinforcement is necessary for confidence in the ability to change. S.H.A.D.E.S. acknowledges, encourages, and is seeking to empower you through giving techniques that may be useful in the transition. People are creatures of habit and find comfortability in a comfort zone. However, is the comfort zone a healthy place to be? Is it of safety? Or a place of escape? Some of the conclusions interjected has been reached and tested in; Clinical Outreach to Childhood Trauma Survivors, those that are Grieving, Domestic Violence Survivors, those who have been afflicted by War, etc. and much of the work has been very successful. In every instance the Survivor had to be taught ways of helping Self without Self hurt. And Others had to be taught ways of helping the Survivors of Trauma and Afflictions without hurting them.

Change is a difficult thing to do if there are hindrances such as secrets, emotional turmoil, interpersonal relationship struggles and polluted environments. There are stages of change that are demonstrated and documented in Prochaska and Di Clemente's work on stages of change and change is a process.

- ➢ Pre-contemplation- a stage just as denial not recognizing the problem
- ➢ Contemplation- a stage when the possibility of change is questioned
- ➢ Commitment and Action- a stage when a decision is made to change the behavior.
- ➢ Maintenance- a stage efforts used to reinforce the change

➤ Relapse- a stage where the possibilities of repeating the unhealthy behaviors.

These stages are the assessment of change and the steps a person takes to make change. It's a model that has been helpful in the Clinical and Business World therefore we can identify it as Personal and Professional.

Another thing that has always been helpful is the Cognitive Behavioral Approach which is a learning model that teaches the individual through recognition of high risk situations. Education is power and with communication and coping skills it can give balance that promotes wellness. Regardless of who shows up behind the S.H.A.D.E.S. the functioning skills are healthy and unhealthy defense mechanisms. S.H.A.D.E.S. themselves is a defense, coping, and survival mechanisms. Some people are known to have Resiliency a quality that many believe is an innate ability to bounce back into shape or position from a situation. And it doesn't mean they aren't wearing S.H.A.D.E.S. to deal with the aftermath of an experience. Nevertheless, they are able to realign themselves quickly. For those that are not endowed with resiliency there is a need to teach coping skills for repositioning. Coping skills are something that is taught and Resiliency an inner resource.

Many of the skills, the Person behind the S.H.A.D.E.S., uses are possibly maladaptive skills. Which means skills the person used at the time was appropriate and needed for their Personal Safety; however, as time went on the skills become unhealthy. For identification purposes in the S.H.A.D.E.S. model it is imperative that the Survivors know though they may feel isolated, ashamed, or different because of the experience, they don't have the only experience. We are going to show they are not alone and want them to become comfortable in knowing the truth. Statistics, Research, and Survivors histories and stories are documented with some of the Maladaptive Skill used in the past and present to escape the pain of the experience. It is important to recognize the Maladaptive Skills are intertwined in the development of the Person behind the S.H.A.D.E.S. Self-Esteem, mental and physiologic states of being are teeters their wellness. There are substantiated maladaptive skills and how they can be defined for example:

- Substance Abuse- Self Repair and altered states
- Promiscuity- Survivors' inappropriate introduction to sex
- Dissociation- separation from experience, unaware, denial, associated with Seat of Passion
- Hostility-Modes of Anger that can become a shield of protection

The substantiated list is longer, however, we are going to use these four that are possibly intertwined with the Maladaptive Skills. Each one of the examples are not only maladaptive but are escape defenses that contribute to Low-Self Esteem. Whether apparent or not, the Person behind the S.H.A.D.E.S. may not have made the connection between their behavior and their experience. The examples substantiate; "They feel some type of way." Survivors must acknowledge is their own maladaptive coping defense so that as they learn new skills and techniques. They must be aware of triggers and slipping back into old behaviors when feeling vulnerable, known as Relapse.

In order to avoid a relapse the Person behind the S.H.A.D.E.S. must identify triggers and plan on ways of handling situations using; communication, self-soothing, and proper diet and nutrition. Triggers are related to high risk situations, people, places, things that are associated with feelings coinciding with the issue. Triggers are reminders that can be viewed as an emotional flashback. Vulnerable relationships make one prone to relapse and are usually amongst family, friends, and cultured communities.

Now it's time to go back to the Journal and identify the triggers that create unhealthy interactions with Self and Others that include people, places, and things. Also identify what the coping mechanisms is used.

NOTES:_____

17 CHAPTER NAME

WORKING WITH OUR BODY

Wisdom is priceless and nothing can be compared. There isn't a Diamond, Pearl, Rudy or a measure of Gold that can be compared. Wisdom lends its potency with guidance to those who are receptive. In touching basis with yourself and making changes it always best to first get a general checkup. Those with medical issues such as hypertension, diabetes, addiction and other health-related problem should continue to work with your physician. And it wouldn't hurt for you to ask that your Cortisol level be tested. S.H.A.D.E.S. chapter "Light Shines Out of Darkness" has enlightened us to the effects of Stress and Cortisol. And "Self Repair" has educated on Health and Family Dysfunction. Anyone seeking to change their diet is strongly suggested that you speak with your physician. Depending on your health status your Physician's recommendations may vary.

Lifestyle change is a major life change that may impact your Trauma. Stress and Trauma can also be the reason for health and weight problems. Everyday occurrences are not always easy to process after trauma and can lead to neglecting Body, Mind and Spirit one way or another. In promoting loving yourself and acknowledging "You" it's important to take a few steps that only you can take. The human body has to be reasonably maintained for it to function properly which includes more than mobility. It requires food that is proportion to meet the needs of the body. The body has ways of rejuvenating itself and maintaining a balance however you have to work with your body. Many people are known for neglecting their body whether its; not eating a well-balanced diet, eating disorders, emotional stress, poverty related issues etc.

Good nutrition is important. It's not just restricted to the body but the mind and aids in controlling some of our emotions. Understanding basic nutrition is the basis for the Body's Health which requires education, awareness and maintenance. Regardless of where you are or who you are, a life situation can take a toll on your body. Therefore, we have to educate ourselves on proper nutrition and other wellness aspects that promote stability in our life.

Nutrition is a contribution to everyday life in the fact that we need energy and other chemicals properties that are supplied through food to survive. The immune systems, vital organs, body systems, all interact with the nutritional supplies for the body. There are essential vitamins, nutrients, minerals, proteins, etc. that are needed to deter some diseases or deficiencies that can be life threatening. It's also important that we not forget the effects of Cortisol and its multiple task in our body.

Proper diet and nutrition further support healthy skin, bones, hair, and teeth. In addition to the fact that the body is an amazing vessel that uses food resources, and body fluids to rejuvenate and regulate the body functions. A balanced diet is so important that in 1992 the United States Department of Agriculture implemented the Food Pyramid. A guide to support and educate the people about what is necessary to maintain nutritional health. There are a variety of foods categorize in food groups that outline serving size and easily affordable resources to get the proper amounts required for nutrients and energy. There are also scientific and medical suggestions that support supplements.

Not to be a Calorie counter but United States Department of Agriculture indicated the recommended and required Calories needed to maintain proper diet, weight, and how to curtail some disease that could impact the Body. Controlling your weight is important because both underweight and overweight people are susceptible to many major medical problems. The abnormalities opens the door for diseases and infections. This is another reason why educational awareness, following physicians advice, and maintaining is important when it comes to working with your body. Calories are recommended in accordance to body size, gender, age, climate (environment), mental and physical functioning.

Establishing various differences brings attention to the awareness of the Calories distributed throughout the body. The energy source for the body is food however the content of energy is measured in heat producing elements known as Calories. In working with your body you burn Calories that is a heating source for the body incorporated in the foods you eat. Gender specifically its best to explore who burns more Calories, how the Calories are burned, and the environmental factors. Included in the necessary body heat are the energy and nutrition resources from the Calories substance.

As we process Routine Activities the body burns' Calories that heat the body and produce energy. Men need more Calories compared to women because their bodies are not as insulated with fat and needs more heat generated by Calories in the winter. Many of us have heard the expression "Burning Carbs" and "Counting those Calories" both being energy sources. Well the two serves different purpose though an energy resource. In capacity younger people participating in sports activities or just functioning in Routine Activities generate energy at a different rate and need more Calories to sustain the body. A construction worker male or female also requires more Calories. Because of the active movement causing the body to burn the Calories. Environmentally factoring a cold geographic place such as Alaska would require more Calories of energy heat than States that are naturally a warmer climate.

When it comes to body weight, we differ in capacity as well therefore; An overweight person consumes more food than the body needs and that excess food is stored as body fat. Underweight people effects are a deficiency of in proper Calories and therefore need to consume food to increase the body weight.

As a reference for better nutrition and eating habits you can consult with:

- Your Physician and a Nutritionist
- Engage in your local community workshops on Healthy Eating
- Access literature from United States Department of Agriculture Calories Allowance.
- Access literature from United States Department of Agriculture Food Pyramid Guide

NOTES:_____

_____

_____

_____

_____

_____

_____

_____

18 CHAPTER NAME

WHO DO YOU "THINK" YOU ARE NOT???

S.H.A.D.E.S. has brought many people through pain and grief and now they don't know who they are, nor their true value. The tinted, darkened, shaded sight with its many shapes, styles, and reasons have taken them outside themselves. There is a thinking pattern that has created a spiritual and physiological composition against the soul. The State of Mind has been altered by the experiences associated with the Pain that they Feel.

The Author/ Writer of S.H.A.D.E.S. lends us a hand in her everyday life and 9/11 experience. She lets us know she has a Spiritual life that subjected various things to her belief system. We all have a belief system and we all believe in something or somebody. Whatever the belief it is strengthens and supports us in overcoming many of the occurrences that life throws at us. Reality is we are Spiritual Beings having a Human Experience that has us processing LIFE. The Author of S.H.A.D.E.S. is Judeo-Christian meaning she has roots in both the Jewish and Christian communities of faith. She believes that about herself regardless of what others say about her it's not what is written in the Scriptures. Though she didn't know for a time she was wearing S.H.A.D.E.S. she did know something wasn't right with the world for the following reasons.

The Author/Writer establishes her TRUTH in her belief that; nothing can happen to you that has not already happened, otherwise the Scriptures would be incomplete. Every experience that has been known to man whether male or female is already written. The response to people, the responses of people and what God has to say about whatever issue it maybe. There are accounts that witness your experience isn't isolated and it has happened to others that probably had the same human response. Therefore you don't have to be sooner one thing than another.

Your experience is real, jolting, and has shaped and styled the view you may have of yourself to certain degrees. Question is; Do you believe everything somebody says about you or do you believe your experience has impacted you emotionally making false evidence appear real? Write your answers in your Journal and the Author/ Writer will write her responses below.

According to the Author/ Writer in the scriptures the Book of Jeremiah (29:11) contains a conversation between Man and God. The Scriptures account is a conversation with the God of his understanding that he serves. The Lord says to Jeremiah "For I know the Ideas that I have in Mind for you, ideas of peace, and the good, and to give you my desires which you will receive to the end."(Paraphrased)

Jeremiah was going through a few things and a few things were up against him. He needed to overcome his adversary with the TRUTH about what God says about him. In another conversation with God, Jeremiah is told: 1:5 "Before you were born Jeremiah, I created in your mother's womb and I knew you then as I know you now. Before you were born, I set you aside as my very own to Speak for Me to the People." (Paraphrased)

There are some things that had Jeremiah upset and he was getting confused with the Time, Experience, and People reactions. Question being; Who is Jeremiah? He is a man separated for God's use in the Human Experience of his Time ordained by God to Guide and

Point the People in the Right Direction. He is a Prophet, He is a Messenger, and He is an Authority over the People. The Messenger Points You in the Right Direction as a situation is NOT as You Know it. Meaning appearance can be tricky. Did the People understand this? Probably not otherwise they wouldn't have been giving him a hard time.

In a Human Experience many may believe things about themselves only because of what has happened to them, what somebody said to them and how people respond to them. All of these occurrences have created issues of conflict with who they are in identity, making what's false appear real. In a nutshell that means people have been lying to them and they have been lying to themselves.

Here's another Scripture that should bring you more TRUTH about you, your experiences and your current identity behind S.H.A.D.E.S. Your circumstances leaves room for questions. Isaiah 54:17; No weapon forged against you shall have worth, every mouth that raises up against you to curse you I shall make to be shown as a liar." (Paraphrased). Therefore S.H.A.D.E.S. has protected you in the experience, that has confused you. It has also shielded you against people that badgered you to the point of Emotional Distress that affects your Self-Esteem. You need to know it is possible to overcome the impact, collateral damage, and know you are an asset. Because you really are strong, you do have worth, and are talented beyond your current understanding of yourself. Your distorted view of yourself has allowed people to extort you while you further extort yourself. This opens the door for EXPLOITATION which is destructive in every sense of the word. Because you are literally being taken advantage of by others and self. Are you really willing to cut your own Self off? Probably not therefore "TO THY OWNSELF BE TRUE".

It's going to take some digging, separation, SELF-LOVE. And here comes those

BOUNDARIES that separate You from Others and Others from You. Low-Self-Esteem exploits, oppresses, burdens and keeps you in BONDAGE with the words and actions of Self and Others. It preys upon the EMOTIONS and SENSITIVE areas of your Life. Others wrongs don't have to be your Rights therefore there is no need to BETRAY yourself because of an experience that has occurred. What you experienced at the hands of another is not your burden it is theirs. And believe it or not you can go on with your life without them trailing behind you. Or reaching into your Personal Life, polluting your Environment with hindrances. The QUESTION 1 remains; *WHO DO YOU THINK YOU ARE NOT?* If you can answer this, you will probably understand why you are here.

S.H.A.D.E.S. will hopefully provide you with some insight in the following questions you could ask yourself. These answers are to be written in YOUR Journal for the sake of your privacy and reinforcing your Boundaries as you engage your Truths.

- When YOU look in the Mirror what or who do you See?
- Who do YOU think you are?
- Who do YOU want to be? **PERSONAL**
- Who do YOU think you are not?
- What do YOU want to be? **PROFESSIONAL**
- Who or what told YOU differently?
- How did it make YOU feel?
- How do YOU value yourself?
- How critical are YOU about yourself?
- Why are YOU so, hard on yourself?

S.H.A.D.E.S. wonders how you faired with these question. Can YOU see the LOVE that YOU are despite the situation and circumstances? Have you considered that though you have been through a few things that behind S.H.A.D.E.S. you are having an identity crisis? Are you afraid of your EMOTIONS? Are you afraid of acknowledging the SELF-ESTEEM?

Hey, what is Self-Esteem anyway that it should be so, important to the person behind the S.H.A.D.E.S. Well it is the Essence of you, the Essentially yours, it's the Core of you, and the Level of what you think and feel about yourself. Emotions connected to Environmental chaos and distortion has afflicted the mental and physiological state associated with thoughts, feelings, and behaviors. The chaos and distortion of view shift the Conscious to an Unconscious State and the Unconscious to a Conscious State. These instances play a central role in Routine Activities of your life. It's like EMOTIONAL impact giving a schizophrenic view of reality.

For example: Scripture writes about another prophet Elijah who had a mountaintop experience where he had the victory. Afterwards Queen Jezebel threatened to take His Life. In the interim of the LIFE and DEATH THREAT, he forgot God had just defeated the enemies and she hadn't the ability to kill him. And as a result of Fear he lost focus on what God did conflicting with what Jezebel said. Things didn't come together giving him two different views (schizophrenic). One of truth (reality) and one a lie that generated emotion stress from perceived danger in false things appearing real. The EMOTIONAL DISTRESS related to FEAR of DANGER overwhelmed his Senses to maintain his mental balance and he became suicidal. Question being: Did he know who he was? Yes, however the experience got shifted when he was threatened with death. Question: Who do you think you are not because of your experience?

REMEMBER:

- We all have the SAME human worth.
- Love is UNCONDITIONAL other tie CONDITIONS to LOVE.
- We have different TALENTS and ABILITIES.
- You experience recreated S.H.A.D.E.S. for your SURVIVAL.
- You have VALUE, STRENGTH, and ESTEEMABLE.
- You are LOVE and have the ability to CREATE LOVE.
- You, the SELF is at the ESSENCE of YOUR BEING.

NOTES:_____

19 CHAPTER NAME

IF ONLY YOU BELIEVE

Faith and Courage has the ability to take you places Hoped for and not seen as in some of the People behind the S.H.A.D.E.S. Courage gives you the support you need to stand and face the shadows of life. If only you believe you can change, you can be healed, and you can recover the Life you desire. There is nothing like living a life with a void, surrounded by confusion about who you are, with unkind feelings tapping and trapping your strength. Could there be something that you are blindsided by and missing?

Every person living, breathing, and those that have passed before us have RIGHTS that can't be taken away. It has been endowed within us. A Gift that takes Precedence in all we think or could ever imagine. That Gift is LOVE. LOVE gives without demanding anything in return. It makes SACRIFICES without grumbling, hurting Self, or Others. It doesn't deceive or emotional blackmail, nor does LOVE falter because it's PREFECT. It's just not received, given, or perceived as PERFECT, because of the way it was introduced. The giver and creator of LOVE is GOD who divinely put you together. LOVE desires all to recognize LOVE especially the LOVE that you are. Just with this BEING said, can the Person behind the S.H.A.D.E.S say; "I AM LOVE" I deserve to receive LOVE", "I can give LOVE" and "I can, and should LOVE myself." Though LOVE is an INALIENABLE RIGHT you still have THE RIGHT TO CHOOSE. Remember LOVE doesn't DEMAND nor is it Controlling. LOVE is unconditional, it has no strings attached and it has no limits.

Problems arise when you lack understanding and knowledge about LOVE. When there are convoluted relationships for lack of BOUNDARIES. When LOVE is exploited, twisted, and debased, with no real outlet for the release of TRUTH about pain or tension. LOVE isn't ever changing into something sophisticatedly perverted. Check the mirror and see if the ENEMY is you because you haven't acknowledged your pain, the desire to be loved, and have not peace to pursue your own happiness. If you are not the ENEMY then it should be easier to separate yourself from your ENEMY. When "Loving your ENEMIES" it was never said that you had to sit and have tea and crumpets with them. Love makes forgiveness a little more comfortable because of the BOUNDARIES. It also allows LOVE to bless you as your enemies see LOVE in you without distorted feeling surfacing.

There are different types of LOVE. Meaning it has many names yet its one in the same. LOVE can differ in relationship without puppet strings. Altruistic Love is the kind that is unselfishly concerned about the welfare of others. Eros Love endorses love in a romantic and passionate conception. Philadelphia Love is the kind of Brotherly love that includes Sisters as it denotes friendship. Agape Love is the kind that goes far beyond appearance because it functions in spiritual capacity. It's a Sacrificial Love that is extended even to those deemed unworthy. At least one of these types is available to you, within your reach, and should be demonstrated in your Life. The truth be told, they should all be available to you and you can receive through various relationships.

There are many MISCONCEPTIONS about LOVE that extend beyond introduction. These problematic misconceptions are behaviors and attitudes induced towards your Fellow-Man. The behaviors and attitudes can bring about conflict in relation to the strong discontent for unwanted actions. These behaviors and attitude of unkindness is what generates your enemy. Nevertheless, if you are willing to separate from the behaviors and attitudes then you can possibly love you enemy from afar. LOVE YOUR ENEMIES don't require you to parlay with them. BOUNDARIES resolve any conflict that would arise between neighbors if; a person avoids doing what they don't want done to them. "Love your NEIGHBOR as you Love YOURSELF.

There are truly Survivors and others people that have discourse and reasoning about God and Love. It is understandable that something or someone has hurt you and caused your pain. It's the behaviors and attitudes of others that has impacted which can cause a person might blame God for human err. And because God didn't intervene at that time, they believe that God is to blame. However, when we examine the relationship that positioned the hurt or hardship people tend to believe God didn't care. Nevertheless, God always cares about how people are treated whether He intervenes at that time or not.

In the publication "BRAGGADOCIO" a Father got angry at God. He blamed God for what was done in God's House by someone claiming to be a Person of God. The Father became angry and stopped speaking to God because of human err. (The Fathers, response is important when seeking to understanding what the Author/Writer means when subjecting experiences to instinctive is literal and instinctual is figurative.) As with the Father in Braggadocio there are expectation of persons with significant positions in relationships. When people that are suppose to uphold the position fail, some of the occurrences can be shocking. Since the behavior is far from what is expected of a person especially in intimate leadership positions.) Nevertheless, in the fullness of time LOVE by Itself challenged and proved He is God and Cared about the Father's entire household.

God always has a reason for not intervening and it's not that the person wasn't in the wrong. God know the difference between right and wrong just as He as a set time and decision made for when He shall judge a matter. Survivors and others might forget from time to time that God has a Household and He holds Court. He judges the actions of His Household first. He is reasonable and takes into account all the circumstances. He is well aware of Family Dysfunctions, Trauma, Mischief and Mayhem.

MONTAGUES & CAPULETS:

The Montague and the Capulet households were no different than the Hatfield and the McCoy. Neither of these families is any different than any feuding family when it comes to cultural perspectives. Love has its principles that outweigh any human perspective that can be placed in position. There are some misunderstandings when it comes to Feuding which are not necessary. Nor is it necessary for you to be misused from a cultural perspectives that are laced with unforgiveness and grudges. You have the Right to Love and be Loved without familial baggage wearing you down. You don't have to allow yourself to be used like a man's house slipper, stretching on both sides. Allowing the slack in BOUNDARIES can cause you more pain than you have ever imagined.

Romeo didn't have to die neither did Juliet for the feuding to end and reconciliations to take place. It was BOUNDARIES and MISCONCEPTIONS that kept the families apart in family warfare. So, what are you killing yourself for? The LOVE of GOD has a way of reaching out to those that have been hurt. He knows how to speak to each and every person and surround them with HIS COMPASSION. Many people wearing S.H.A.D.E.S., and using Self Repair are comforted in LOVE by LOVE. God knows exactly what type of balm is needed to support your health, safety and healing.

12 STEPS CHANGES: *AFFIRMING BOUNDARIES IN LOVE*

LOVE isn't going to write out the 12 Step lifestyle changers, but is going to share Itself. Many people don't understand the importance of the Spiritual component in the Steps themselves. The 12 Steps are Spiritual Principles that when adhere to has the ability to remove affliction and change the way you think about yourself, others, and the way you live your life. Not following them to the best of your ability can change you and your life from one thing or another. Maintaining yourself with the Spiritual Principles helps you to avoid some of the pitfalls of the past. There should be a conscious awareness of these pitfalls and various courses of action to take.

The senses of a 12 Stepper due to the Honesty about behaviors, attitudes and feelings can warn them of danger ahead. The Steps provide an alternative path especially when the bridge is out and there must be a detour. More over a Stepper will know when the bridges are beyond repair and they accept the reason why. Not only do the Steps improve your Spiritual capacity they promote; physical, mental, and emotional well-being that give balance to an otherwise chaotic life or areas of life.

Amongst 12 Steppers are those that struggle with LOGOS (reason) whereas some are sure of God; which is Love, some are unsure, and others don't believe. However, there are those that didn't believe that have come to their senses. The reality that "The Steps" can change their life and remove afflictions made an impact. Those that don't believe have accepted God as Good Orderly Direction. They recognize "The Steps" work and acknowledge the process of healthy change in Self and Others. These are Steppers choosing to make a change that helps them along life's journey.

There are many 12 Step Anonymous groups that vary according to affliction and the desired lifestyle change. Many of the Steppers have come to believe they cannot change on their own. They have come to the end of Self and accept they need guidance and insight. They are willing to live a healthy productive life, and help others with the same willingness. They accept that they are not perfect, have made mistakes, and are willing to do their share in making the amends. They understand boundaries regarding personal safety and the confidentiality of others.

Many have a Sacrificial Love that covers others regardless of where they are because Grace reveals itself in Love. Spiritual maturities that accompany them living in Spiritual domain keep's them clean of resentments, un-forgiveness, and acceptance of life on life terms that doesn't require they cheat themselves or burden others.

There is a lot of LOVE in the Principles and the Steppers only difference is some are more mature than others. Some have taken death defying leaps of Faith and are willing to share the experience as well as help others overcome. Humility functioning in LOVE blocks humiliation, misconceptions, and deceptions.

The S.H.A.D.E.S as we know introduced itself with intense emotional pain, physiological changes and stress. Beginning to Love yourself will open you to new realties and gradually remove the hindrances or affliction of your view. Yes, the lenses will lighten up. S.H.A.D.E.S. are removed, lightened, and recovering sight is a process, not an event. Therefore everything can't be done at once. One of the major things, that will be dislodging is the emotional intensity, but the residue of Emotions will rise and can become conflictual. The residue must be addressed to avoid triggering past behaviors and attitudes based on an undercurrent of feelings.

Therefore awareness is key, boundaries are necessary and letting LOVE carry you through the process. Some Survivors know that Trauma changes a person's perception on life. LOVE is gentle as you work these things out with help. Don't forget to be honest, faithful, and don't betray yourself or forget LOVE when the change comes. LOVE, trumps all things. Thankfulness opens windows that foster a relation with God, Self and Others, therefore don't forget the affirmations, and try new skills.

NOTES:_____

_____

_____

_____

_____

_____

_____

_____

_____

_____

20 CHAPTER NAME

IMAGINE THAT HUEY

S.H.A.D.E.S. has colored the world of the person behind the S.H.A.D.E.S. in different tones. Some tones are emotions and some are delightful hues that make life more of a comfort. There is a body of language and expression that are released through colors that are cultural and scientific. Studies on Colors and the effects on Emotions is a progressing field amongst the psychology of color. However, how a person emotionally responds to color is subjective in nature. And the feeling one person may have for a color might not be the same for the next person. Therefore, feelings, moods, and behavior are going to differ and are also cultural based in meaning and value. Because the personal nature of Colors that can influence a person hasn't a strong scientific backbone its viewed as sketchy.

Nevertheless, colors has substance associated with psychological, physiological, emotional and performance in an environment. Which takes us to the connection with relaxation, a place of peace and personal space of the Sanctuary. Sometimes a person is powerless over the color décor of an environment and sometimes they are not. Therefore, learning about the effects of Colors on a person's emotions can be supportive from a S.H.A.D.E.S. perspective.

Since colors can cause negative and positive emotional stimulation the impact for a Trauma Survivor is important. Colors can stir the emotions and feelings from the calm, cool and peaceful to anger, fear and hostility. While colors have different meaning to people, Survivors and Ordinary People want to be in comfort during Routine Activities. Colors that are defined in its cultural aspects in societies can be as powerful as the emotions. The

S.H.A.D.E.S. society can promote their personal and professional welfare through grasping colors.

Throughout the S.H.A.D.E.S. manual the Author/Writer uses Empirical Research and the Webster Dictionary for several reasons. It's simple, easily accessible, and gives meaning to the definition. It broadens the horizons with various depths that COMMUNICATE and VALIDATES the view behind the S.H.A.D.E.S. It builds up the INTELLECT, UNDERSTANDING, and changes the PERSPECTIVE in subtle ways. It SHAPES and gives INSIGHT to the SURVIVOR EXPERIENCE as DEW for the SOUL.

DEFINING COLORS:

Webster Dictionary indicates: The sensation resulting from stimulation of the retina of the eye by light waves of certain lengths. Any coloring matter; Dye, pigment, and paint which when mixed in various ways, produce the secondary colors. Black, white, and gray are often called colors (achromatic colors). Black is caused by the complete absorption of light rays, white by the reflection of all the rays that produce color, and gray by an imperfect absorption of all these rays.

COLOR LANGUAGE AND EXPRESSION: The Colors, they Speak.

Outward appearance or semblance; Plausibility; appearance of truth, likelihood, validity, or right; justification (i.e. the circumstances gave color to his contention) a general; character (the color of his mind) to give a pleasing, convincing, or reasonable appearance to; make plausible; to alter or influence to some degree, as by distortion or exaggeration (prejudice colored his view).

JOVAN~KA CONYERS....S.H.A.D.E.S.

This is the defining in the context of the Webster Dictionary however to piggy back on Color and S.H.A.D.E.S. the Webster SYNONYM caption reads: Color is the general term for which we see the definition above. SHADE refers to any often graduation of a color with reference to its degree of darkness (light shade of green); HUE, often equivalent to COLOR, is used specifically to indicate a modification of a basic color (orange of a reddish hue). TINT refers to a gradation of a color with reference to its degree of whiteness and suggest a paleness or delicacy of color(pastel tint). TINGE suggest the presence of a small amount of color, usually diffused throughout (white with a tinge of blue).

In the context of the above defining meaning there is captivation in S.H.A.D.E.S. And Webster meaningful substance takes us a step further with finalizing COLORABLE that is said to mean: Capable of being colored; apparently valid or plausible, but actually deceptive. Therefore the person behind the S.H.A.D.E.S. world is color coated in a way that defends that which has distorted their view of a dangerous, unacceptable, painful experience, yet the defense mechanism harnesses the truth. That's why they wear S.H.A.D.E.S.

S.H.A.D.E.S. and Colors both can have a POSITIVE and NEGATIVE response on the MIND, EMOTIONS, and ENVIRONMENT. Wearing colorful clothes that make you comfortable has been one of the suggested requests from the Author/ Writer. It's a matter of getting arrayed and looking in the mirror and saying , "What a view!" The use of Color can aid your emotional well-being as well as those in an environment. In building your Sanctuary of PERSONAL SAFE SPACE colors should be considered. Colors can be used in meditation and for maintaining a focus. Colors are used to stimulate and influence the environmental body as they are sensation producing a stimuli response. Specific colors have specific effects on the emotional and mental platforms.

Colors communications to us in ways many probably haven't thought about. Not even those that have the task of street marking that are designed to communicate to other workers. Communication is involved in repairing the underground pipes, plumbing hazards, or reconstruction. Prior to ground breaking someone has the responsibility of surveying and applying the necessary color codes. There are 4 basic color coded indicator outlining the streets;

1. BLUE- indicates water   2.RED-indicates electricity   3. YELLOW-indicates gas

4.ORANGE- indicates cables.

These basics as we can see has the ability to cause extreme problems and threats of danger for members of the community if accidentally ruptured. However, the people behind S.H.A.D.E.S. aren't necessarily clearly color coded but that doesn't stop the world of their perception from being very comfortably colored. The reason the Author/ Writer is implementing colors because of the effects the colors contribute to mental health and moods. This doesn't mean that people behind S.H.A.D.E.S. won't oppose some color because of what they represent to the S.H.A.D.E.S. experience. Colors are further associated with CHARACTER and IDENTIFICATION; everyone knows about Royal Receptions and the lavish display. But let see what some colors speak too. Our defining color schemes comes from various resources and from the experiencing perception of the Author/ Writer who as we recall is our model wearing S.H.A.D.E.S.

After an extremely stressful experience, loss, or threat beyond one's belief system can be challenging. The Author/Writer's felt shattered by the exposures and experience of situational abuse and trauma. Her perception has been coherently arranged in a designed order that identifies, sorts, and connects information in a mosaic ensemble of life and self. These bits and pieces can be arranged to reflect emotionally weak and physically strong from a mental capacity. However, when it comes to Colors the ones she gravitated toward had personal meaning and cultural value. And were also used to produce a more relaxed state of existence in identity. Past and present research has been able to uncover the ability of Colors to be instrumental in (Holistic) healing, mediation and recovery. There are Color Psychologist that use a therapeutics of Chromo therapy which is color psychology. This is a practice that has been around for centuries and used in ancient cultures. In CHROMO THERAPY colors are used as an alternative treatment and the purpose are specific. Some examples are:

RED: used as stimuli for the body and mind and promote circulation.

ORANGE: used to heal the lungs and promote energy levels

BLUE: to promote comfort during illness and pain treatment

As said previously Colors are defined in accordance to personal nature, culture and experience of a person. Therefore a person may have a more in-depth meaning and identity to colors that are correlated to behavior and physical health.

ORANGE: communicates a stimulating sense of comfort, action, liveliness. It's one of those radiate colors that rejuvenates and promotes a healthier well-being.

RED OR SCARLET: Has a connection to blood, atonement, drunkness, violence, and persecution. However the color is instrumental in stimulating clarity of mind that produces physical strength that helps the immune system.

PURPLE: Speaks of Luxury, Royalty, Kings, Queens, and Riches befitting or associated with a Supreme Being. People behind S.H.A.D.E.S. can feel compromised until their self esteem is invoked.

VIOLET: this is a color combination that is strongly acquainted with spirituality and is healthy when maintaining a balance. It has the ability to support you in a faith building belief system. It's imperative to understand what is practical and what is not to avoid extreme behaviors. Spiritual knowledge can be applied in practical ways without endangering self and others.

BLUE: dictation of heavenly character, a calmness functioning of tranquility that comes with reflection and rest. Heightens self -esteem as one releases the dignity acquainted with their life, self worth and empowers their motivation.

YELLOW: pronounced as breath of life to many cultures around the world. It's brightness invigorates. The vigor provides light and has a positive impact on the nervous system, it's a stimulus to thought and communication.

GRAY: one of the unusual colors we have as it is not a standalone color it is brought out by other colors. Just as in the areas of life it represents the imbalance, the unclear, it stands in separation of. The color positions and indicates a midway place of decision that lays in wait for clarity. Once the space is clear the gray in- between two extremes generates the substance that products a desired outcome.

BLACK: mystery, calamity, sorrow has a positive negative response because of the three mentioned associates. The color and related indicators such as mystery, calamity, and sorrow that could be acquainted with grief. Mystery could be referred to the untapped resources in the life of the person behind the S.H.A.D.E.S. that has been covering their inner strength.

WHITE: denotes the fine linen of cleansing, purity, serenity, and righteousness that can indicate victory or surrender for completion of an expected end. Whether victory or surrender it relays the ability to move on in destiny. Therefore surrender shouldn't be identified with defeat but letting go of an ongoing struggle in order to move forward. Surrender should be more or less equivalent to humility.

GREEN: has the depiction of a harvest in life and privileges that are grounded in growth and balance. The nature of one's own life is to grow and prosper in various areas of life.

BLENDS: these are colors created through the mixing and blending of other basic colors. The Survivor's perception can represent a colorful perspective of how they view the world.

Imaging and the Imagination is a creative aspect in the sense of life after the experience. The reasons for using colors in this manual are for; self esteem building, help with grounding, devoting time for personal growth, and empowering motivation. Recovery is a process and using colors is a technique that requires some instructions.

There are other forms of Mediation techniques and skills that can be incorporated in the simplest of ways. Take health and fitness that suggest the importance of a proper diet for wellness. Food can be soothing but over eating is not the answer nor are empty calories that are meant to satisfy Emotional Distress. The same colorful mediation can be used to maintain the proper diet and portion. Some food colors stimulate the appetite and therefore one should be mindful of intake. Fruits and vegetables are providing color and nutrition to help with balance. It does the body good.

NOTES:

21 CHAPTER NAME

HEALTH AND FITNESS

Preventing Relapse entails learning new coping skills that produce and motivates change as it reinforces the ability to promote growth. Health and Fitness are a very important part of maintaining MIND, BODY, SPIRIT. It's important to learn how to manage STRESS, EMOTIONS, and ANXIETY that could cause one to tip the scales one way or the other when it comes to BALANCE. There needs to be a conscious level of security for managing your health for the release and reduction of stress. When speaking on balance there is no need to seek for perfection, we are seeking stability. There are processes and stages to the Life Experience that require a conscious effort. Essentially some of the basic needs in health and fitness are:

➢ Proper Diet and Nutrition

➢ Sleep and Proper Rest

➢ Exercise and Wellness

➢ Healthy Self Soothing Techniques

For the most part these are the Precursors to aids in relapse prevention, recovery that stimulates, and recapturing the time behind the S.H.A.D.E.S. Wellness isn't soliciting perfection or perfect health. It's about balancing your emotional life and physical health. Working with your body has its goal in helping you eat right to avoid the Self Repair Methods that cause improper weight loss/ gain. And being mindful of calories that don't promote emotional health but support the overwhelmed stress. Health and Fitness facilitates the precursors to bring you out of an exhausted state into renewable energy. However you must find a balance between: MIND, BODY AND SPIRIT. The collaboration will give you Inner Support for dealing with external conflict. Therefore the essential of Sleep is as necessary proper diet and nutrition.

FORTY WINKS:

There are times when you may go to bed only to wrestle with the bed sheets, tossing and turning. Or you get up in the morning just as tired and weary as you were when you went to bed. Throughout the day everything is not as clear, you are not as alert, and your body seems sluggish. Reality is you are not functioning to your full capacity because you need rest. What's missing is rejuvenating SLEEP. Rejuvenation that gives necessary energy that clears the body and mind of stress and sharpens the senses.

Sleep is one of those essentials with defined characteristics in life that is processed in stages. One-third of a person's life is spent in SLEEP which is an altered state of consciousness. It's an influential function to human life. In both the mental and physical life it boost the immune system. It increases creativity and creates dreams as it adds to the ability to problem solve. Dreams are an important part of memory that is a function in the cerebrum located in the brain.

In avoiding relapse and incorporating new coping skill of a conscious state the body needs rest. Those that have gone to bed in an upset state know the effects of emotional imbalance can making them weary. There is a difference between SLEEP and REST; the only way you can get rest is if you get adequate sleep. This takes some explaining for greater understanding of the happenings that occur during sleep.

Sleep has FIVE different STAGES that are cycling through the time spent in the

ALTERED STATE of CONSCIOUSNESS. During these five stages the body experiences inner environmental changes that work with the organs and body agents. REM (rapid eye movement) SLEEP is the most IMPERATIVE taught about in coping skills, relapse prevention, and healthy sleep cycles and patterns. However how do we get to the REM SLEEP stage? As previously mentioned sleep is within stages and cycles that take you into restfulness to rejuvenate the MIND, BODY, AND SPIRIT.

In the SLEEP STATE you lose awareness (consciousness) to the external environment surrounding you in the WAKE STATE that would STIMULATE a response.

- STAGE 1 of the cycle effect's internal physiological environment of the body and slows the pulse, relaxes the muscles, and creates a circular movement from one side of the other of the eyes. The Sleeper is easily awoken to the external surrounding environment (noise). This stage generally endures only several minutes.

- STAGE 2 of the cycle is known as the deep spindles state that takes you into a deeper sleep state. In this cycle rhythmic burst begins short brain wave activity.

- STAGE 3 of the cycle is known as delta where slow waves are activities that reach a high peak. This stage emerges and interacts with the deep spindles state in stage 2 The Sleeper isn't easily awoken to the external stimuli surrounding of the environment. Internal physiological environmental changes in the body continue to slow and decrease the blood pressure, body temperature, and heart rate.

- STAGE 4 of the cycle the brain continues activity using delta waves and the internal physiological environment of the body reaches its lowest level. The blood pressure, body temperature, heart and breath rate are low however internal environment of the body is stable during the night.

It takes about an hour to reach to stage 4 after which the cycle goes backwards from 4-1. The cycling of stages takes place all during the Sleep state and takes about 35-40 minutes. Throughout the sleep state the internal physiological environment change there is an increase and decrease of the blood rate, body temperature, heart rate, and muscles are more relaxed in the stage 1 cycle making the externals of the surrounding environment therefore arousal from sleep state is even more difficult. The sleeper state is deeper and REM Sleep in process.

> **STAGE 5** of the cycle is the REM state sleep where brain and physiological function though its responses are of those in an awakened conscious state. The stage doesn't last that long approximately 10-15 minutes before cycling the NON-REM STAGES 2, 3, 4, and stage 1 is now REM 1 for the sake of understanding. The Sleeper experience several stages as the REM STATE becomes longer and longer and NON-REM STATE shorter and shorter. The estimated time is a 60-90 minutes in duration of the cycling patterns of REM to NON REM that occur 3-6 cycles during the SLEEP STATE. The stages occur over and over again repeatedly through the Sleepers sleep state.

All other stages are NON-REM sleep before cycling into different stages and back again that eventually disappear. The REM STAGE of sleep are also in cycling stages yet this is believed to be the state where DREAMS occur. This is not to say that in NON-REM state that you don't dream because the Sleeper dreams in NON-REM also. The REM sleep states cycle vary over time in accordance to age over time.

It's has been averaged that a person get 8 hours sleep for rejuvenation of physical and mental functioning. The lack of proper rest slows the response time, memory is altered in forgetfulness, judgment and reasoning is impaired, and behavior could be erratic and unpredictable. The behavior substantiates the lack of SLEEP and REST creating WEARINESS when you are EMOTIONALLY IMBALANCED.

Any Environmental impact that is perceived as a threat, negative, or shocking conflicts with the generated STRESS related to the body and surroundings. Whether it's from the internal or externals of the human body or the surrounding of the human body there is an impact. Therefore awareness, proper diet, proper sleep, effective communication is necessary for stability and creativity. The person behind the S.H.A.D.E.S. will be experiencing emotional stress as they gradually use the cognitive abilities to change. Change is neither an easily thing nor are the things connected to the S.H.A.D.E.S. easy to accept.

There are other BODY AGENTS that are chemical messengers that assist with a healthy SLEEP STATE. Chemical messengers are called NEUROTRANSMITTERS that SPEAK to each other. The COMMUNICATION is important to the EFFECTIVENESS for BALANCE. Sound's like the everyday effective communication that is used to support Self and Others to determine how our needs are met. Another thing in common is the way the messengers can overlap in various areas of responsibility, just as in the HUMAN COMPOSITION that function without our knowing. Some BODY AGENTS such as Neurotransmitters, Hormones, and other chemical messengers are effective in influencing Memory, Mood, Emotional Balance, Learning Abilities and the SLEEP STATE are examples of the Speakers and messengers.

Serotonin is a chemical messengers that function with other chemical messengers that support the SLEEP STATE in aiding the conversion to MELATONIN, a Sleep Hormone. Whereas, GABA messengers are giving support for SLEEP, SEDATION and RELAXATION. These are the BODY AGENTS responsible for BODY DEFENSES released from the BRAIN.

NOTES:

22 CHAPTER NAME

I FEEL SOME TYPE OF WAY

S.H.A.D.E.S. has educated, made suggestions, and opened doors for promoting EMOTIONAL stability that has locked many people behind the tints and designer lenses. It has all been leading to this vitally important stage of acknowledging and getting in touch with our feelings and expressing how the person behind the S.H.A.D.E.S. feels.

There are strong FEELINGS entangled within the EMOTIONS that generated the S.H.A.D.E.S. They are associates of extreme stress, loss, and threats of violence. Remember violence comes in many forms that can have an astronomical effect on how a person feels about Self and Others. S.H.A.D.E.S. is positioned on the bridge of the nose can be interpreted as supportive. They can also be polluted and deluded. People, places and thing including you may not be clear about reality. This would also imply that you are not clear about you. For instance violence in a verbal form may leave a person feeling bad about self and lacking in confidence. EMOTIONALLY they depend on the very people that are hurting them and blocking them from seeing their full potential, which is processed over time.

Underneath the blocked vision there is HURT and PAIN in the form of; ANGER, FEAR, GRIEF, SHAME, GUILT, ANXIETY etc. The false allusions appearing real overshadows these EMOTIONS, making them unnoticeable. The unique thing about the overshadowing is that the emotions are usually grasping and griping both sides of the fence.

For example a Survivor and a Perpetrator may both be griping SHAME at different angles creating a scissor look. In other words the arm of shame being held is angled in a way that the Survivor is holding the Perpetrator side and the Perpetrator is holding a Survivors side of the fence. A visual of arms crossed one across and on top of the other. This type of angle opens the door for victimization on the Survivors side from both Perpetrator and Self.

Question now is whose shame is this? One thing we know is the Survivor is not responsible for their personal assault and should neither carry the SHAME, BLAME, nor GUILT. Also, what type of DENIAL is this? And finally what type of emotional scars does this type of violent lesions leave? If the person behind the S.H.A.D.E.S. is unaware they will carry the load which is not theirs to bear. Therefore, they move through life behind S.H.A.D.E.S. overwhelmed with Shame, Guilt, Anger, and an assortment of misdirected mixed emotions. This could be a very depressing state to resign one's life expectation too without thought of the Self-Destructive nature.

Previously we discussed in the Human Composition portion that Emotions are part of who we are as a person. Emotions for all intended purposes of truth and accepted knowledge in Mind, Spirit, and Body that the Emotions are the Spiritual. They are forces and energy of the Mind that sits at the seat of the Soul. Don't get this wrong Feeling are valid they are the portions of the Emotions that connect the person to awareness of the Emotions. Yet there is affect that sets the tone of the emotions. When characterizing the tone it's just as the tinting of S.H.A.D.E.S. tony, tony, tony…in propensity. Therefore we have some feeling that are stronger than others in intensity such as Anger.

Let us focus with our knowledge, understanding, and tools that have been implemented. The Author/ Writer's history with S.H.A.D.E.S., and Trauma shows how Perpetrators perpetuates Violence in her life. Therefore, before you begin take a few breaths, review triggers, and denial in S.H.A.D.E.S. And use the journal to write down points that connect to your feelings. In this S.H.A.D.E.S. Manual this could be the hardest and toughest part. It's like coming up the rough side of a mountain and climbing from the bottom or midway, it will take commitment. It shouldn't be rushed and has to be done over time at a steady pace that doesn't cause you to slip back into a pit of pain. Communication would be most effective in dealing with this portion of S.H.A.D.E.S. Some parts of Life will begin to make sense, other parts of your Life will become clear, and Boundaries for personal safety may have to be established, reinforced or realigned.

FREEDOM OF EXPRESSION

S.H.A.D.E.S. has to bring back a few key aspects that help the person behind the S.H.A.D.E.S to build on communication and knowing you have and always had the right to express yourself.

"Assertiveness" you open the door to healthy relationships, communication and maintain your boundaries. Knowing your Rights taps into various areas of your Life and Relationships. Culture, Tradition and perceived Family Trust could be only equated with Betrayal and contradict your Rights to Express Yourself.

- ♠ You have the Right to Speak for yourself and put yourself first at times.
- ♠ You have the Right to Say No when you really want to say No; not yes
- ♠ You are human and have the Right to err
- ♠ You have the Right to step against criticism
- ♠ You have to Right to Change your mind
- ♠ You have the Right to express your opinions and stand in your convictions

- ♠ You have the Right to intervene on behalf of Self to clarify what you mean
- ♠ You have the Right to Emotional, Spiritual, Social support and ask for Help
- ♠ You have the Right to choose
- ♠ You have the Right to feel and express your pain

These are some of the Rights you have and need to know when it comes to your welfare and security. Though there are times you will hear things and not like the Criticism, however be clear there is Constructive Criticism. In times of Constructive Criticism it's in your best interest to Listen, Probe what's being said and then acknowledge what's for you and what's not. Constructive Criticism is for the purpose of Improvement. If you Reflect on why one uses a COACH as in why someone participates in S.H.A.D.E.S., it's only for sharpening your abilities for Personal or Professional growth. There will be conflict within your life and attitudes that you can't change in other people only in yourself. Learning to NEGOTIATE and how to FIGHT FAIR which IS healthy in communicating your needs and foster relationships without breaching boundaries.

INALIENABLE RIGHT:

KNOW THE DIFFERENCE BETWEEN HOLDING HANDS AND CHAINING SOULS.

Every person living, breathing, and those that have passed before us have RIGHTS that can't be taken away. It has been endowed within US as a people and a person. The Gift takes Precedence in all we think or could ever imagine. It's an INALIENABLE RIGHT that can't be transferred or taken away as in a piece of land or property because it is a part of who you are. However, you can give and receive the GIFT without losing it or pieces of yourself. That Gift is LOVE.

There are many misconceptions about LOVE because of the way it has been shared, received, and exhibited. There are different types of LOVE, there is something you can't do with LOVE, and there are things that LOVE by Itself can challenge and prove.

First start with what you can't do with LOVE and the main reason you misunderstand Love. LOVE is unconditional, it has no strings attached and it has no limits. Perhaps, now we can move onto some other facts about LOVE's giving and receiving. It has already been mentioned that there are different types of LOVE. Meaning it has many names but is one in the same though differing in relationship without puppet strings.

LOVE gives without demanding anything in return. It makes SACRIFICES without grumbling and hurting Self or Others. It doesn't deceive or blackmail, nor does LOVE falter because it's PREFECT. It's just not received, given, or perceived it's PERFECT to many. The giver and creator of LOVE is GOD who desires all to recognize LOVE, especially the LOVE that you are. Just with this BEING said, can the Person behind the S.H.A.D.E.S. say; "I am LOVE" I deserve to receive LOVE", "I can give LOVE" and "I can, and should LOVE myself." Now that you know, LOVE is an INALIENABLE RIGHT, you still have THE RIGHT TO CHOOSE. Remember LOVE doesn't DEMAND nor is it CONTROLLING.

ROMEO & JULIET: *AFFIRMATION*

How do I love thee, let me count the ways...... LOVE

I have absolute and good will concerning you...

I endowed you with spiritual pieces of myself...

I am unselfish towards you and am an object of affection...

I look beyond you faults and supply your needs...

In compassion I feel your pain and hurts...

I am gentle and merciful toward your survival...

My passion for you is stronger than any fear you have...

I am intimately involved with you no matter how you see our relationship...

My love for you does for you what you cannot do for yourself...

I express myself in your joy, peace, patience, meekness, longsuffering, and faith...

I am filled with goodness and I am gentle therefore in Love and Justice I surround you...

I am sure to overcome and endure, not forsaking you in many ways regardless of your feelings.

Since, LOVE has shared with you and your RIGHTS have been made clear take off those Grave Clothes. Blessed are those who mourn.

GRIEF:

Grief is a perplexing intense sorrow associated with Brokenheartedness caused by the loss of a loved one or something that has caused a great unhappiness in one's life. Grief has many layers of emotions connected to the sorrows, gaps in coherence of the happening, and fragmentation of Life. S.H.A.D.E.S. blocks the intensity of pain associated with grief. Not only is there sorrow, there is Anger, Denial, Fear, Lack of Trust and multiple matters that all pertains to the brokenheartedness and feelings of Betrayal.

Recognizing loss, denial, expressing Anger, and overcoming fear, can rebuilding trust in

Self and Others. Opening up to mourn and facing the Broken heartedness, that has caused you such hurt, helps you to reveal the LOVE that you really are. Acceptance and Love are the keys to moving on with your life. Change isn't an easy thing as said before "we are creatures of habit," "we are emotional being," "we are socially and emotionally" connected to various interpersonal relationships. And some reputed areas can be a TOXIC energy source that is drowning your INNER SPIRIT.

It's okay to be angry, nevertheless, it's not okay to be unable to express that anger in a healthy way. It's okay to let go of those that are hurting you, betraying you, or hindering you. Letting go can also mean living your life with boundaries that keeps perpetrators of your pain at a distance. It doesn't mean that you don't love them. It is necessary for your own personal safety, happiness, and your process.

Remember you are not obligated to be a slipper, door mate, and you have the right to love, care, and provide for you without feeling guilty, or infringed upon. You have a right to loving relationships and to express your likes and dislike. These are just the things that the MONTAGUES and CAPULETS failed to understand concerning Romeo and Juliet who took their own lives in crises.

The journal is there to help you confront some of the emotions and distress hidden behind the S.H.A.D.E.S. Making the release will help you open doors for yourself and you at some point will be comfortable to share that pain with others. Its okay to cry from the outside oppose to the inside. Tears are a good cleanser for the soul and you release that which has keep you emotionally blinded or bound. Bottled emotions are TOXIC emotions.

Fear of starting over without lots of Emotional Baggage has stopped, distorted and stagnated your progress in life. It is possible that you may begin to think about the Self you have neglected. It's okay to, appreciate you, treat yourself, hugs you and admit that you love yourself. Some good memories related to the Loss of a Loved Ones can be helpful. Would they really want you to live your life in the Shrine you built on Interpersonal Relationships? Would they not want the best for you? Would they want you to live a life that is not Honorable? When it comes to the loss of a Parent this can bear down on a child as Parent who has loss a child. However there is no greater sorrow than the grief a parent when there is a loss of a child.

Don't go overboard and maintain your balance by using the coping skills and communication skills suggested. Monitor those triggers, watch your diet, don't take on too much in one session, don't allow anger to consume you or denials to embattle you, pursue your newly emerging Self with Personal Safety.

Once you break through denial the first emotion that might present itself is Anger. It may show up subtle, aggressive and within intense rage, use the journal not harmful substances, or act on the feeling. Call for help, write it out, because the feelings once sorted out will pass. LOVE hears your prayers, mediation, affirmations and stabilizes your course. You are on a journey out of your past and you are evicting things and people who had a choke hold on your life to Rest.

NOTES:_____

_____

_____

_____

_____

23 CHAPTER NAME

BREAKING POINT

It's now time to reveal some relapse prevention techniques and discuss what worked for who. Environmental changes and the clearance of toxicity can support a Survivor with relaxation, therefore, we will also explore some other techniques that can be helpful for some.

Aroma therapy would also be a helpful suggestion however there is safety and sensory connection to the technique. To be most effective, essential oils should be pure and uncut. Oils should never be kept in plastic containers. Traditionally, essential oil are stored in amber or blue glass to protect them from ultraviolet lights. They should be touched on the body with cotton or an eyedropper. Placing the finger directly on the bottle opening can alter the purity of the scent within.

- ♠ Cedar-Dispels sluggishness, lethargy
- ♠ Cinnamon- Treats fatigue and depression
- ♠ Eucalyptus- has a cooling influence; helps with anger
- ♠ Frankincense- Maintains meditation focus; inspirational and rejuvenating
- ♠ Geranium- Has an uplifting vibration; addresses anxiety
- ♠ Jasmine- "Softness" the emotions;' treats listlessness, fear
- ♠ Lavender- Aids memory and alleviates mental stress; old- fashioned headache remedy
- ♠ Neroli(Orange Blossom) Counters, insomnia, nervous tension

- Patchouli- Clarifies problems; encourages objectivity; member of the lavender family
- Pine- Lessens claustrophobia; elevates emotions
- Rose- Functions as an antidepressant; effective for grief
- Sage- Supports healing processes, the purification of space
- Sandalwood – Evokes confidence and supports meditation overall

*** Oils can present with a matter of money however there is an alternative to some fresh air solution. King pine an everyday off the grocery store shelf can be helpful and cost effective. It is a housecleaning product that has the ability to elevate the emotions.

FIRE SAFETY PRECAUTION:

Aroma therapy and candles are soothing for some individuals. Please use the following safety precautions. If you plan to use candles as part of your relaxation skills please establish the guidelines of safety.

CANDLE SAFETY CHECK LIST:

- Never leave a lit candle unattended.
- Never leave children and pets unattended with candles burning.
- Never place candles close to flammable materials, such as Christmas trees, wrapping paper, kitchen cabinets, draperies, bedding, clothing and furniture.
- Always maintain a one-foot circle of safety with a burning candle.
- Make sure the candle sits properly in the holder and won't fall out.
- Make sure the candle holder is stable and sits on a flat surface

  S.H.A.D.E.S. is in strong agreement with The White Barn Candle Co. and the New York

City Fire Department with safety concerns; Candles must be used with extreme caution. Candles must never be left unattended. Be sure to keep out of reach of children, pets and drafts. Take care to remove all packaging, labels and accessories before lighting. Burn only on heat resistant surfaces. Keep melted wax pool free of wick trimmings, matches and debris. Avoid burning around things that catch fire easily, such as potpourri, and centerpieces.

***As an alternative to fire lit candles for oils that are electric oil burning devices that can cost somewhere in the neighborhood of $10-$20. Or you can go without either the fire or electric burners and use a glass bowl able to sustain boiling water and add drops of oil. The bowl must be position safely to avoid anyone becoming scalded or burned by accidental spill of the contents.

NOTES:_____

_____

_____

_____

_____

_____

_____

_____

_____

_____

24 CHAPTER NAME

EXERCISE FOR WELLNESS

We've discussed BODY AGENTS, TOXICITY, NUTRITION, and SLEEP the things we need to promote good health and wellness. These are starts to changing the view of the person behind the S.H.A.D.E.S. When speaking of WELLNESS it for the purpose of creating a BALANCE that is supportive of your stability. There is a need to reflect upon the human composition all 14 mentioned and the divine (Holiness) within BODY, MIND and SPIRIT. Each and everyone one of us is wonderfully made. Our belief systems and cultures may be different but everyone has the same human composition. We all have a BODY, MIND, AND SPIRIT. It has been mentioned and discussed and can't be implemented enough that we are not aiming for perfection only balance in our lives.

During the lifetime of the person behind the S.H.A.D.E.S. their Body has been exposed to violence of different kinds. What the MIND can't accept from the overwhelming emotional experience created an imbalance. The stressful emotions from the internal and external environment AFFECTS impact the body. When S.H.A.D.E.S. took control unnoticed the environmental assault left a door open for stressors. These stressors have drawn the person behind the S.H.A.D.E.S. deeper into a tinted, shapely, dim-lite space possibly through Self Repair. The internal and external environments are now polluted with things that are not a part of you and are exhibiting themselves as character defects.

In other words you weren't born this way, a way in which you are unable to process life.

Or unable to develop within various stages of personal and professional growth. Now it's time to reshape your path by telling your story. The realignment of your path requires new techniques to be incorporated for the purpose of coping with Routine Activities. Some of those stressors will be cleared away through healthy living that includes exercise. *IMPORTANT:* consult with your physician to determine your abilities as an individual and follow the instructions prescribed.

EXERCISE DOES THE BODY GOOD

There is true sayings: "To be aware is to be alive." Awareness breeds life into a situation therefore by no means should the person behind the S.H.A.D.E.S. be reckless. It is important that you set the goal and submit yourself too, a good a physical checkup. Follow the physician's recommendations and be honest with the physician about the idea of incorporating EXERCISE into your daily living. If you are given limits, follow the physician's instruction because it's an aid to you restoring your physical and mental health. Again this is about BALANCE NOT PERFECTION. Because balance and wellness is not the same in essence for every person behind the S.H.A.D.E.S.

For example you are not to deter from any specified diets or medication because they are prescribed to balance your wellness. The physician probably will prescribe you specific exercises you are physically fit to perform without hurting yourself. If you are taking counseling with a mental health physician it's okay to speak to them about S.H.A.D.E.S. because it enables them to SUPPORT you within the TRANSITION as they learn more about you and your experience before and after S.H.A.D.E.S. The support reinforces the internal and external walls of the PERSONAL SAFE SPACE, BOUNDARIES, EFFECTIVE

COMMUNICATION, and STABILITY. **REMEMBER:** SUPPORT is incorporated within your RIGHTS as a PERSON with or without S.H.A.D.E.S.

EXERCISE has been acknowledged as a healthy support to the human internal and external environments of the body. Some people are health conscious and some are not while other are engaged in exercise for other reasons. The consciousness could be because of Self-Esteem, Sports Activities, and for health reasons. However many people are unaware of the genuine support the BODY, MIND, and SPIRIT is receiving. They are as oblivious as they are to the neurotransmitters and other BODY AGENTS engaging their physical and mental state.

Exercise helps in the DETOXIFICATION of the TOXIC BODY AGENTS as they clear the bloodstream and exists through some of the body organs. Certain STIMULI is generated in the activity of exercise. When we search the definition of Exercise afforded through the Webster's Dictionary for a defining point that is easily understood from any point of view. Webster writes:

EXERCISE- performance of duties, functions, etc activities for the purpose of training or developing the body or mind; systematic practice; esp. bodily excretion for the sake of health. a regular series of specific movements designed to strengthen or develop some part of the body or faculty; to put the body, a muscle, the mind, a skill, etc into use so as to develop or train; to exert control, influence, authority etc; to engage attention and energy about a decision.

Therefore we clearly see that our defining points of good health, physical and wellness are supportive of a Lifestyle change. When assess the types of exercise one could practice:

- walking, jogging, running

- stretching, pumping iron
- dancing, yoga
- use of a series of gym equipment with a regiment

These are just options that can be used to support the goal of using proper exercise to counteract the effects of stress. There are other BODY AGENTS at work that have the ability to promote a conscious state of Good feelings. Those behind S.H.A.D.E.S. that have compromised themselves through substance abuse, low-self-esteem, suicide, promiscuity and other unhealthy behaviors of escape were seeking the imitation of Good feelings.

The body has what is known as Endorphin that release Good Feels and they are further healthy Stimuli that can promote good health through proper exercise. Proper Exercise and Nutrition also support the SLEEP STATE, MEMORY, EMOTIONAL STATE, REDUCES STRESS, REJUVENATES, ENERGIZES etc. Which demonstrates a needed for healthy decision making choices. There are other BODY AGENTS that can malfunction when there is an unbalance within the internal and external environments. Whether the Body or Physical dwelling place. The UNBALANCE STATE could cause depression and other emotional impairment created in the mental health state. This could cause a person to put themselves in harm's way when they normally would respond with a SAFE, HEALTHY, REASONABLY decision.

For instance Dopamine, Serotonin, Acetylcholine, Norepinephrine and Epinephrine, Amino Acids, GABA and a host of other BODY AGENTS known as Neurotransmitters are affective and responsible for influencing mood and cognitive states. There is BODY AGENTS that further support the immune system and have some active involvement in maintaining stress levels.

NOTES:

25 CHAPTER NAME

FORGIVENESS:

Reconciling your life, repairing damage, and experiencing a new found freedom includes forgiveness. You have to take action in forgiveness while setting Self and Others free. This is no easy thing for many people nevertheless, understand it's a process. You have to know how to approach the course of action. You have to sort out your feelings and value as well as what matters and doesn't. Only the person behind the S.H.A.D.E.S. can deem what matters and what doesn't. It's their experience, feelings, and perception of what's relevant. And determine if it's healthy or unhealthy internally and externally. Another reason is because they have to become aware of the possible toxicity.

Resentments, revenge, malice and all manner of unhealthy decision could and will keep them in a place of despair. One could suffer from Emotional retardation, sadistic, convoluted behaviors and attitudes that are extremely unhealthy. These are responses related to Emotional Toxicities that are contrary to a healthy person's well-being. Underpinning the emotions promotes neurosis when there is no emotional release. You have been hurt by someone or hindered from Self Expression, and have feeling behind a loss. Ultimately a person could and most likely would hurt Self and Others whether intentionally or accidentally because of an Emotionally stronghold. Forgiveness is a form of release of toxicity, baggage and pain.

The Author/Writer of S.H.A.D.E.S. wants to extend an apology to those that have been traumatically concealed. And to those who have suffered a loss that nothing can be compare with. Yes, your pain is real and your sorrow is true, nevertheless you have accept what you are powerless against.

CASE AND POINT: Death and Dying made the Author/Writers life a living nightmare. She was powerless to change what Death had done and sought Self Repair Methods to escape the reality. Death changed her life in many different ways exposing her to victimization, abuse and more of his actions. She began to believe Death to be a violent individual and difficult to understand. She couldn't grasp the reasoning behind him and that reaping tool.

Most profound is the way she suffered at the hands of Perpetrators and Peepers after Death passed by. There were actions and decisions that proved to be costly and unmerited once Death had come and gone. For the Author/Writer it was like a quiet storm and a big mess of violence. After a while she began to believe she lived in the shadows of Death for some reason not known to her.

Though she was saddened and angered by Death actions she was willing to forgive those that assaulted her after he passed. Her willingness to forgive kept her going though she has had a hard time with the process of forgiveness. She has gotten as far as talking to GOD about Death. And telling GOD how hard it is to forgive the same people that just keep doing harmful things at the same time. It gives clear meaning to **DEATH, VICTIMIZATION AND TWISTED REALITIES.** Nevertheless she is willing at some point-in-time and continues to struggle as while moving on.

Violence as we previously have stated comes in various forms and degrees. The Author/Writer S.H.A.D.E.S. were generated through shocking and stress experiences related to Death and Dying. Not every person response is the same whether out of resiliency or other coping skills mechanism. In some cases it's just a matter of acceptance after breaking through denial. A person can know the truth nevertheless be unable to handle the truth of an experience as with the Author/ Writer traumatized state.

Remember the stages of change. And just the thought of consideration of forgiveness is a step in the right direction. "Willingness" contemplation stage and steps of action is an acknowledgment of being willing to unleash You from Others and Others from You. There is no you holding them in a grip and you are free. Forgiveness is no pieces of cake; there are both internal and external environmental factors. Some feelings have been internalized where they should have integrated on a healthy note. When it is all said and done, the issues, the feelings, the people, places, and things, a Survivor may come to the conclusion that they may have to forgive their entire past.

We can now go back to reinforce the new techniques and work through the process of forgiveness. There will have to be an assessment of all you have discovered to know when and how to forgive. The Love and Joy will help accomplish this important stage of growth together. The journey through the process of forgiveness can be difficult, nevertheless, a dash of willingness will support you with the process that changes your life. Prochaska and Di Clemente has prepared you for the process of change. Therefore give yourself room and space to grow and note the changes.

NOTES:_____

_____

_____

ABOUT THE AUTHOR

Jovan~ka Conyers born and raised in the Bronx developed amongst many Survivors of Childhood Traumatic Experiences and Adult Traumas. She has an extensive history of Self Repair and has been extremely misunderstood in the Clinical and Legal Societies. Her misinterpreted history effected a multitude of dimensions creating and imbalance that ultimately hindered her Personally and Professionally. For lack of an understanding amongst many her children and family were directly impacted in the struggle. And regardless of pitfalls and trap doors she continued on the Survivors path wearing S.H.A.D.E.S.

Moving forward, shifting and flowing she continued to advocate for Self and Others in plain view of those who were positioned as Supportive Agents (Peepers). Her family and the families of other Survivors effected by trauma kept her motivated on her journey as she grew in her Judeo-Christina Faith. S.H.A.D.E.S and the next few publications express her experience and support for the Community of Survivors. She has a publication on the Amazon **"BRAGGADOCIO"** that is strictly written in trauma. Unfortunately because of continue victimization the book was published in an "As Is" condition. Which means the book is understandable though it is unedited.

We must acknowledge Survivors as a Community......S.H.A.D.E.S. is written in an educational format with an open forum to stimulate hope and support for the welfare of Survivors.

S.H.A.D.E.S

SHADES HELP ADJUST

DANGEROUS EXPERIENCES

FOR SURVIVORS

www.ingramcontent.com/pod-product-compliance
Lightning Source LLC
LaVergne TN
LVHW081357060426
835510LV00016B/1878